LITTLE BOOK OF BIG IDEAS

Politics

This Modern Books edition published by
Elwin Street Productions.

Copyright © 2007 Elwin Street Limited

Conceived and produced by
Elwin Street Limited
144 Liverpool Road
London N1 1LA
www.elwinstreet.com

Illustrations: Richard Burgess, Emma Farrarons
Designer: Thomas Keenes

ISBN-13: 978-1-906761-22-6

Printed in Singapore

LITTLE BOOK OF BIG IDEAS

Politics

Anne Perkins

Contents

Revolutionaries and Nation Builders

Great Leaders

Introduction

Politics, the relationship between man and the society in which he lives, is as old as mankind. Politics is at work in any group of people, organisation or institution. This book is offered as an introduction to the politics of nations, although many of the ideas in it apply to both smaller and larger units.

Politics looks for answers to questions about who should make laws and why they should be obeyed, what principles they should observe, and what ends they should achieve. Described in the simplest terms, political ideas tend to fall to one side or the other of the authoritarian–libertarian divide, a continual search for equilibrium between the need for order to ensure the stability of a just society, and the individual desire for – and right to – freedom. God has sometimes been taken to be on one side, sometimes on the other.

The development of political ideas has largely been an evolutionary process, each theorist building on, modifying or responding to the work of predecessors and contemporaries. The weight attached to different questions has varied according to the circumstances of the time. Following the chaos of civil war, political theory tends to focus on maintaining order; following years of rule by an elite, it tends to highlight the legitimacy of dissent.

Major changes in social order – such as the rise of Christian Europe, the first Islamic empire, the Age of the Enlightenment, or the Industrial Revolution – produce new ideas about the relationship between the governed and the governors, between the obligation of citizens to obey and the origin of their rights to behave as they please. Rulers and rebels alike have always looked for legitimacy in the work of political theorists, and those theorists and their accompanying propagandists have always supplied the politicians with ideas to serve their purposes. Sometimes the propagandists have articulated ideas with such clarity that, like Edmund Burke or Tom Paine, they become associated with them forever. Sometimes, like Lenin and Marx, the leader and the political philosopher have become so inextricably entangled that a whole new thesis arises.

The particular group of theorists and leaders on these pages has been chosen both to highlight the work of the founding fathers, of Plato and Aristotle, Locke and Montesquieu and Marx, and to shed some light on the ideas shaping the politics of the 21st century. The ten themes are or have been the motivating forces of turning points in world history. They have all left an indelible mark on the world in which we live today. The empire builders and conquerors, revolutionaries and leaders, are also men and women who were influenced by and in their turn influenced the work of the political philosophers, and helped draw the political lines across which our own politicians debate. The leader is often the coda to the development of an idea over centuries – the brilliant improvisation, or the glorious (or inglorious) finale.

There might have been dozens of others. Perhaps this Little Book will provoke the reader to make their own list.

Anne Perkins

Plato

Plato's political investigations sought a state that enthroned wisdom. He argued that politics was an elite activity suited to a small group of highly educated individuals. His ideas have been used for centuries to justify dictatorships and oligarchies.

Born: c. 427 BC, Athens, Greece
Importance: Promoted government by an elite band of philosopher-statesmen
Died: c. 347 BC, Athens, Greece

Plato grew up during the long decline of Athenian power, a period of great political turmoil during the course of which his teacher, Socrates, was unjustly condemned to death and Plato himself was forced to flee Athens. On his return he founded the Academy, in effect the first university, as a center of intellectual enquiry into a wide range of subjects. Education was Plato's abiding interest, and towards the end of his life he tried (unsuccessfully) to turn the new king of Syracuse, Dionysus II, into the kind of philosopher-king that he believed was essential for good government, a mission that nearly cost him his life.

Around 378 BC, Plato wrote his great political work, *Republic*. Based on a series of dialogues between his original master, Socrates, and a group of distinguished Athenians, the work tried to explain the recent ill fortune of Athens and examined how to reverse the decline. Plato was concerned with justice, which to him meant enabling individuals to fulfil their purpose as nature had intended. Plato saw society divided into tiers, at the peak of which was an aristocracy of philosophers. Each tier was constrained by the obligations of its function, so preventing excess. According to Plato, an elite band of philosopher-statesmen was needed to lead the blind – the ordinary citizens – to the good life that they cannot even imagine, itself a reflection of the ideal state, a static and harmonious whole.

This exposition of rule by an elite is sometimes seen as a first defence of a 'party', a political grouping united around rational 'scientific' doctrines, working in the interests of the people but not answerable to them. In the 1930s it appeared to rationalise the kind of totalitarian rule that became familiar in Soviet Russia. But Plato, while prepared to impose a kind of communistic life that even excluded family ties in order to sustain the state, understood the weakness of his own utopian vision: it relied on the actions of his utopian aristocracy being moderated by their obligation to act with wisdom, and Plato acknowledged the improbability of this.

Plato's later work, *Statesman*, proposed that the rule of law should bind leaders to right principles. Finally, in *Laws*, he searched for a way of enforcing a system that acknowledged the moral frailty of the individual while creating the circumstances in which the ruler could rule. His answer was rigorous education for citizens governed by a hierarchical system of councillors at the summit of which sat a secret 'nocturnal' council, the 'sheet anchor of the state'. Plato never lost his faith in the need for a small, enlightened group to lead the masses to the light but his abiding contribution to the development of European political thought was the idea that the state existed for a moral purpose.

Aristotle

Aristotle, student of Plato and tutor to Alexander the Great, is the founding father of Western political science. From Plato, he took the ideas of a moral purpose for the state but shifted the balance in favour of the citizen and democracy.

Born: 384 BC, Stagira, Greece
Importance: Championed government by the majority for the majority
Died: 322 BC, Chalcis, Euboea, Greece

Aristotle's *Politics* was written towards the end of a life devoted to devising rational systems. The work was a mixture of ideas about, and definitions of, the constitution of the ideal state – one whose purpose was the good of the whole community. This partly philosophical exercise was informed by an analysis of real states, both contemporary and historical. Like Plato, Aristotle believed that all things had a purpose, and that a human's was to be good. His quest was in organising society in such a way that people were able successfully to reach their full potential – educated, rational and self-aware. The *polis*, or political world, that Aristotle preferred was the intimate environment of the city-state. 'Man,' he famously declared, 'is a political animal', living alongside others, distinguished from animals by the power of moral judgment and the ability to communicate ideas of right and wrong. The ideal state would unite its citizens for their common good. Yet, as nature is infinitely varied, and animals fulfil a range of functions, people too would serve different functions according to their capacity in pursuit of this overall end. Some, the aristocracy, were capable of higher achievements than others. And, although most slavery was unjust, some individuals were fit to be no more than slaves, in need of the guiding hand of a more able master.

Like Plato, Aristotle believed that the rule of law – the rule of God and reason – was the necessary precondition to a successful state. 'Passion perverts the minds of rulers, even if they are the best of men,' he declared. Therefore the law must take precedence over the individual. The state, too, is greater than one individual, yet it must be able to reflect the wishes of its citizens. Aristotle's analysis of 158 real examples of government led him to conclude that different forms fitted different circumstances. He categorised states according to the number and virtue of those exercising power. An individual ruler was either a 'monarch', who governed in pursuit of honour, or a 'tyrant', who sought riches. Government by a minority might be a 'noble aristocracy' or, if corrupted by the pursuit of wealth, an 'oligarchy'. Government by a majority, in the common good, was 'polity'. But 'democracy' was mob rule. Aristotle's ideal model was a monarchy, but since corruption of the best produced the worst – tyranny – he concluded that polity, the least good of the three types of government he identified, also happened to be the least bad when corrupted. Therefore, government by the majority for the majority – with impartial justice and mutual respect between the rights of rich and poor, hierarchical and slow to change – was the form most likely to produce and sustain the good life.

'One should call the city-state happy, not by looking at a part of it, but at all the citizens.'

Aristotle

A thousand years after he died, Aristotle's ideas were rediscovered in medieval Europe where they were employed to undermine arbitrary and tyrannical rule. Although some of his ideas, in particular the emphasis on an elite, are now rejected, his thought still frames contemporary debate.

Niccolò Machiavelli

Machiavelli stands apart from mainstream political philosophy, in that he addresses none of the questions about the nature and origin of authority or the purposes of government that preoccupy many of his predecessors and successors. Instead, he was concerned with strength, stability and security.

Born: 1469, Florence, Italy
Importance: Challenged the idea of the state existing for a moral purpose
Died: 1527, Florence, Italy

Niccolò Machiavelli was born into a family traditionally associated with the administration of the great Renaissance city of Florence. At 29 he became a leading counsellor to the Republic. The return of the Medicis to Florence interrupted his career from 1512–1521; during this turbulent period, Machiavelli wrote both his major works, *Discourses on Livy* (1531) and *The Prince* (1532), though neither was published until after his death. By 1527, when Rome fell to Charles V, Machiavelli was distrusted by both the Medici and republican camps in Florence, and, again denied a job, died.

Discourses on Livy and *The Prince* are Machiavelli's two enduring works – the first, a long, thoughtful attempt to translate the success and mitigate the failings of the Roman republic in the contemporary era; the second, a brief, unscrupulous account of how to hold and wield power successfully. In their secularism and their republicanism, they are the founding works of modern political philosophy. Even now the impact of Machiavelli's cynicism can shock: 'Men are so simple and so ready to obey present necessities, that one who deceives will always find those who allow themselves to be deceived.'

In *The Prince*, Machiavelli is not seeking rules for a moral utopia but a practical answer to the problems he saw around him: a violent and insecure world, capable of being mastered only by a strong ruler whose success rested on glory in battle. Virtue in a prince is not goodness (though it might be presented as such) but effectiveness, indifferent to moral outcomes. Thus 'one cannot call it virtue to kill one's citizens, betray one's friends, to be without faith, without mercy, without religion' – unless circumstances demand it. To be great, a prince must win victories not just over rivals but, through valour and audacity, over fortune itself.

In the early 16th century, the Church, corrupt and quarrelsome, stood in the way of a united Italy, while, Machiavelli thought, Christian ethics sapped the character of the people—disastrously, since the character of the state depends upon the character of its citizens. His ideal state is not a monarchy (as the word 'prince' might suggest) but a democracy, in the elite sense of the word. In a democracy, rival groups could be held in tension with one another within the law, united by a respect for the state itself.

Once corrupted, Machiavelli thought democracy almost impossible to restore. The worst form of ruler was the prince – like Caesar – who could have preserved freedom but instead destroyed it. In the 20th century he might have condemned Hitler but admired Stalin; at a time of chaos, tyranny could be justified if it led to the restoration of stability.

Within a generation of his death, the idea of a state that did not exist for a moral purpose was beginning to win acceptance, and successors like Spinoza and Rousseau (see pages 18–19 and 24–25) respected him as a republican and a democrat.

Political power: The ability to influence the behaviour of others within a society. The centralisation of power advocated by Machiavelli runs the risk of corruption, so many societies divide power between branches of government – traditionally executive, legislative and judicial – which balance each other out to prevent abuse.

Thomas Hobbes

Both in his development of the idea of the 'state of nature' to explain the origins of society – and justify absolute power – and in his belief in expediency as a sufficient motive, Hobbes was profoundly influential through the 18th and 19th centuries.

Born: 1588, Wiltshire, England
Importance: Introduced the concept of a covenant under which all surrendered their rights to a sovereign
Died: 1679, Derbyshire, England

Thomas Hobbes graduated from Oxford at 20 and began a long and fruitful association with the noble Cavendish family. Through them, Hobbes was able to tour Europe, learning, first-hand, of the explosion of scientific knowledge that was transforming mankind's understanding of life. His greatest and best-known work was *Leviathan*, published in 1651. Two other important works preceded it: *Elements of Law* (1640) and *De Cive* (1642), published in English as *Government and Society* (1651).

Like Machiavelli's (see pages 12–13), Hobbes's political philosophy was a response to war, with the aim of creating a strong and stable society. But Hobbes had absorbed the scientific method: he looked for fundamental laws by which people were shaped and sought a scientific base for a political system to accommodate them. 'The skill of making and maintaining Commonwealths . . . consisteth in certain rules, as doth Arithmetique and Geometry.'

At the same time, his hypotheses were framed by the rise of the nation-state. The quest was for a kind of government that could bring peace and stability not to a few hundred citizens in a city, but to hundreds of thousands across a wide territory.

Leviathan, his examination of mankind in society, was startling at the time for the slight role it awarded to God and for the bleak picture it painted of people without government. He

Above: Members of the family, the clan and the city-state all chose to give up personal rights in return for the security of rule by a strong leader.

envisaged a person's natural state as, in effect, a state of war. In this condition, Hobbes famously declared, life was 'solitary, poor, nasty, brutish, and short.' In direct contradiction of Aristotle, he denied that man was a political animal. Humans acted only from self-interest and sought power as a means to indulge their will more freely. Hobbes thought individuals had no rights at all except the right to life and, hence, self-defence. Ultimately the right to reject one authority in favour of another could only come about when the first authority could no longer offer security.

Hobbes proposed a mythical covenant by which the people gave up all their rights in order to rescue themselves from the anarchic state of nature. Here, the 'sovereign' (which might be an individual or an assembly) had absolute power; he decided the law, what was taught and the nation's religion. Although subjects were bound by the law in their relations with one another, the sovereign could dispose of his subjects' property as he wished. It was an arrangement that mimicked the order of the family, nature's social unit. Hobbes's state had no moral function: it was simply the most efficient way of imposing and sustaining order.

Hobbes's secularism and realism were a stark contrast with contemporary thought and set the terms of the argument for the next 200 years.

Libertarianism

Libertarians argue that a government's principle objective is to preserve individual freedoms and only to preserve them. These freedoms are usually summarised as the right to life, liberty and property. A debate as to the extent of state intervention necessary led to the divergence of liberalism and libertarianism.

The notion of inalienable rights originated in a defence of the individual against the state. Liberalism is, in effect, a debate about the proper limits on government in a society of individuals who are 'self-owners'. Thomas Aquinas (1225–1274) held that government authority was limited by God-given individual rights; no mere temporal ruler could ignore the individual without breaching divine law. In the 17th century, John Locke (see pages 20–21) argued that the state's power was limited by rights originating in a 'state of nature' where rational man understood that his own rights to liberty and property depended on observing those of others; government was established by consent in order to protect them. In the 19th century Jeremy Bentham argued that rights were consequential, tending to produce the greatest good for the greatest number. According to John Stuart Mill, that led to the 'tyranny of the majority'. Minorities also had rights that had to be protected.

In the first half of the 20th century, a sharp divide developed in liberal ranks. The revival of classical liberalism led to the introduction of the term 'libertarianism' to distinguish the purists from those who had softened their line. Progressive liberalism – represented in government by Franklin Roosevelt in the United States and David Lloyd George in Britain – was a response to the inequalities generated by free markets that left millions in poverty and insecurity. It greatly expanded the activities of the state. In

1941, Roosevelt set out what he called the 'Four Freedoms'. To the familiar freedoms of speech and worship, he added the freedom from want and the freedom from fear, notions that, for the next 40 years, underpinned American liberal government.

More classical liberalism revived in the work of political economists like Austrians Ludwig von Mises and Friedrich Hayek in response partly to the experience of communism and totalitarianism in Europe. They restated John Stuart Mill and Adam Smith's warnings against interference in the basic freedoms. In particular they warned against constraining the market by welfare and employment protection. In the long run, through the operation of spontaneous order, they said, the market itself would even out disparities. They argued that individual charity was more efficient than state welfare.

In the 1950s, Isaiah Berlin described two kinds of liberty, 'negative' and 'positive' – that is, liberty as the maximum possible absence of restraint regardless of the effect on social justice, and liberty as a good that requires intervention to avoid despotism by the rich.

There are also left-libertarians who try to embed the pursuit of egalitarian objectives, in particular the ownership of property, which they argue in nature is held in common, within more conventional liberalism.

By the early 21st century, libertarian ideas were widely influential in the developed world, adopted as integral to the thinking of most right-of-centre parties. But there is growing evidence of a rediscovery of a more traditional liberalism, that once again promotes the merits of community and society that coexists with and modifies the rights of the individual.

Baruch Spinoza

Benedictus Spinoza was an early rationalist. Like Thomas Hobbes (see pages 14–15), he sought a scientific basis for his philosophy, but for Spinoza, people should not be the creatures of their passions – they can use reason to liberate themselves.

Born: 1632, Amsterdam, the Netherlands
Importance: Argued for liberty of conscience—for individuals to be allowed to think for themselves
Died: 1677, the Hague, the Netherlands

Spinoza was born in Holland to well-to-do Jewish parents. Although raised Orthodox, he was also well educated in secular ideas; he was a follower of Descartes, also living in Holland at the time. His early questioning of the Bible's grasp of the laws of physics earned him a period of excommunication. During this time, he supported himself by lens-grinding while trying to formulate a system that would embrace his growing vision of man and nature. By 1662, he had written *A Short Treatise on God, Man, and His Well-Being*, *A Treatise on the Correction of Understanding* (*Tractatus de Intellectus Emendatione*, published 1670), and the first book of his three-part masterwork, *Ethica*. He died of consumption, still a young man. After his death, his *Tractatus Theologica-Politicus* and *Tractatus Politicus* were published.

Spinoza, doggedly pursuing his own logic, argued that since all creatures – animal and human – follow their natural laws to the limits of their powers, subject to their reason, and that since God is in everything, everything man does, therefore, is Godly. Sceptic Pierre Bayle later called this a 'monstrous hypothesis'.

Spinoza's most significant contribution to political thought is his argument for liberty of conscience – initially intended to advance religious freedom, but later applied more generally. It is drawn from his conclusion that people are governed by natural law – that is, the law of their nature, not derived from any other authority. They have a natural right to follow their nature, and in doing so, form opinions about right and wrong. It is therefore a breach of natural law for anyone else to try to dictate to them. 'A sovereign is thought to wrong its subjects, and to usurp their rights, if it seeks to tell them what they should embrace as true and reject as false. . . . For in such matters an individual cannot alienate his right even if he wishes.'

'Peace is not an absence of war, it is a virtue, a state of mind, a disposition for benevolence, confidence, justice.'

Spinoza

Spinoza greatly underestimated a person's ability to allow someone else to do their thinking for them, and he accepts that, although it is a right, it does not prevent a sovereign treating someone who thinks differently as an enemy. It would, however, be unreasonable, since Spinoza believes the purpose of government is more than Hobbesian security. Rather, its purposes are peace and the freedom for individuals to think for themselves. 'A commonwealth whose peace depends on the apathy of its subjects, who are led like sheep because they learn nothing but servility, may more properly be called a desert than a commonwealth.'

Paradoxically, Spinoza's belief in tolerance, intended to accommodate God, led him to be considered atheistic by some of his contemporaries and pantheistic by some successors. His ideas were neglected for a hundred years after his death but were eagerly rediscovered by 19th-century utilitarians and remain a subject of philosophical study.

John Locke

John Locke was the first philosopher of the Enlightenment and a theorist of liberal and constitutional democracy and individual freedom. Locke's liberalism was initially used to justify a very limited form of democracy and constitutional monarchy. Yet his ideas about the nature of labour, property and individual rights were subsequently the basis of much more radical doctrines. Traces of Locke can be found in the US Constitution and linger in the work of Karl Marx (see pages 38–39).

Born: 1632, Somerset, England
Importance: Promoted the idea of a liberal and constitutional democracy, and individual freedom
Died: 1704, Essex, England

John Locke was born an Anglican, son of a country lawyer who fought for the Parliamentarians in the English Civil War. In Oxford from 1652 to 1665, he preferred the rapidly developing experimental sciences to the conventional curriculum. He acquired the support of the future 1st Earl of Shaftesbury, Lord Ashley, whom he helped draft a constitution for the US state of Carolina, granting freedom of worship but banning atheists. Fearing persecution, from 1675 to 1679, he retreated to France, where he was influenced by the empiricist Pierre Gassendi. He returned to England before fleeing again, in 1683, to Holland.

After the Glorious Revolution in 1688, Locke returned to England in the retinue of the future Queen Mary. His two treatises on government were probably written to celebrate the revolution. This is the period in which the English constitution was made, and Locke, the Whig Party's leading thinker, was at the heart of its development.

The first of the treatises was intended to refute the divine right of kings, by which every monarch was supposed to be the Biblical Adam's descendant. Locke dismissed this as an absurd thesis. Like many of his contemporaries, Locke envisaged that man had once lived in a state of nature; but it was very different from Hobbes's – a 'state of liberty, not a state of license', governed by the law of nature, which required each to respect the 'life, health, liberty, and possessions' of others.

Locke's state of nature was intended to explain the rights that he wanted to prove government was obliged to protect. So in a state of nature, people lived in 'a state of perfect freedom to order their actions and dispose of their possessions and persons as they think fit, within the bounds of the law of nature . . . a state also of equality, wherein all the power and jurisdiction is reciprocal.'

In order to prosper, individuals made a social contract, establishing a government with the power and the right to make laws in the public interest. The only rights given up were the right to judge and to punish. The rights to property and to freedom of thought, speech and worship were all retained.

> 'All mankind . . . being all equal and independent, no one ought to harm another in his life, health, liberty, or possessions.'
>
> Locke

Locke – who examined each of Aristotle's categories of government (see pages 10–11) – thought the form best suited to preserving individual freedom would be mixed: an elected legislature, with executive powers wielded probably by a single person, the monarch. He wanted legislative and executive powers held separately, an idea more influential in the United States than in Britain.

'His ideas,' Bertrand Russell wrote of Locke, 'were so completely in harmony of those of most intelligent men that it is difficult to trace their influence.'

Charles de Montesquieu

Through his great work, *The Spirit of the Laws*, Charles-Louis de Secondat, Baron de La Brède et de Montesquieu, inspired the Declaration of the Rights of Man and the US Constitution and influenced Russia's Catherine the Great.

Born: 1689, Bordeaux, France
Importance: A leading influence on the Declaration of the Rights of Man and the U.S. Constitution
Died: 1755 Paris, France

Charles-Louis de Secondat was a minor French noble who inherited the barony of Montesquieu, the name by which he became best known. His reputation was as a dilettante, so it was to general astonishment that he published his first work, *The Persian Letters* (1721), an amusing dissection of Parisian manners, the Roman Church and the French monarchy written in the form of a dialogue between two Persian travellers.

In 1727, he was elected to the Académie Française and set off on the Grand Tour of Europe. Much impressed by the English constitution, he analysed it in what became *The Spirit of the Laws*. Anticipating Edward Gibbon's famous work by 50 years, he also wrote *Reflections on the Causes of the Grandeur and Decline of the Romans* (1734), an original analysis of how the very success of Rome led to its destruction. For the next fifteen years, he devoted himself to preparing what became *De l'Esprit des Lois* (*The Spirit of the Laws*), finally published in 1748 to huge acclaim.

Eschewing the classic categorisation of governments by where power lay, instead he decided they were distinguished by how they used their power, an 'animating principle'. So a republic (which might be democratic or aristocratic) was maintained by the people's virtue (public spirit), a monarchy by honour and despotism by fear.

The section based on his English experiences was a development of Locke's theories of the separation of powers: legislature, executive power and above all the judiciary (to preserve the rule of law) should each be a separate entity if liberty was to be preserved. These were the ideas eagerly taken up in America twenty years later, even though – influenced by conservative opinion in Britain – Montesquieu had greatly overstated the separation of powers in the English constitution.

The most original aspect of his work, perhaps eccentric at the time, was his discussion of the effect of external factors on institutional development (arguably making him the first sociologist). In primitive societies, he believed climate was a powerful force – one of many factors bearing on the citizen that the legislator had to contend with. He also identified other, 'secondary causes', such as religion and laws that played a greater role as civilization spread. He identified religion as a social phenomenon, finally liberating the state from God.

> 'The spirit of moderation should also be the spirit of the lawgiver.'
>
> Montesquieu

His book was duly condemned by the establishment and placed on the Vatican's index of banned books, giving Montesquieu the opportunity to write *Defense de l'Esprit des Lois* (1750) and finally, an elegant contribution to the new *Encyclopedie*, *Essai sur le Gout*, or *Essay on Taste*.

Montesquieu's ideas circulated widely; his description of the complex interplay of many factors on laws and customs was recognised in particular by Edmund Burke (see pages 30–31), who used it as a powerful argument against revolution.

Jean-Jacques Rousseau

Rousseau, philosopher of romanticism, transformed attitudes to political theory with his revolutionary idea that 'man is born free but is everywhere in chains'. Summed up as '*liberté, egalité, fraternité*', his ideas became the battle cry of the French Revolution of 1789.

Born: 1712, Geneva, Switzerland
Importance: Contributed to the idea of individuals surrendering their rights under a social contract.
Died: 1778, Paris, France

Jean-Jacques Rousseau's life was as unorthodox as his political theory. His first great work, *Discourse on the Arts and the Sciences* (1750), set out the essentials of his philosophy: individuals were essentially good but had become corrupted by society and civilisation. His second *Discourse* (1755) dealt with inequality, the roots of which he found not in nature (although there are differences between individuals) but in the earliest moves toward society. Although society enjoyed at first 'a golden age', soon love produced jealousy, rivalry, competition and pride. Fatally, property followed, and then law and government to protect it.

In 1762, he wrote *The Social Contract*, describing how liberty might be regained within society, with its famous opening: 'Man was born free, but he is everywhere in chains.' He argues that individuals are shaped by their social circumstances. Liberty, Rousseau thought, could be found in a society where all individual wills are pledged to form one moral, 'general' will, devoted to serving the common interest and distinct from the sum of individual wills. He wished to devise a society in which individuals would prosper, and yet his ideas appear to give succour to totalitarianism.

As in Hobbes's philosophy (see pages 14–15), a person gives up all rights in return for civil rights gained within society, making

Left: Rousseau believed that each citizen should submit his individual will and be ruled by the 'general' will of the common interest.

'a total surrender of each associate with all his rights to the whole community'. He claims that a society motivated only by the common interest will make just laws: within them, humans can be 'forced to be free', because obeying the general will is the same as obeying individual will. This complete rejection of the rights of individuals is one of the most problematic aspects of his thought and was abused to terrifying effect during the French Revolution.

Recognising that inequalities were not restricted to property, and that the masses might not be clever enough to meet the demands of living in a just society, Rousseau borrows from Machiavelli the suggestion that a little deceit might usefully be used to inspire obedience – for example, a claim to divine inspiration.

Rousseau's ideas about society and about religion – he found Christianity, though truthful, inadequate for the purposes of his ideal state – forced him into exile. *The Social Contract* was banned in Geneva and France and for years Rousseau was a fugitive. For a time he lived in London, with a pension from George III, before returning to France in 1768 and marrying the woman who was probably his first mistress and also the mother of his five children. He continued to write prolifically, including his autobiographical *Confessions*, published posthumously.

Feminism

Feminism describes not only a philosophy but a cultural, societal and political movement. In its narrow political sense, feminism is the struggle to achieve institutional and economic equality between women and men. But understanding of that equality is influenced by both the cultural and the sociological context.

The position of women has been questioned in the West ever since political theory was taken away from the patriarchal Church. In the 18th century, the enthusiasm for liberty and equality espoused in the works of Locke, Paine, Rousseau and others soon extended to the role of women. It was Mary Wollstonecraft who first demanded that society, if it was to allow men the full expression of their reason, should recognize the rights of women too.

But although gender equality acquired powerful philosophical support in the 19th century – from John Stuart Mill, for example – and women's inferior legal status became a theme of some of the era's greatest writers, it was only when feminism became focussed on the demand for the vote that it became a political force.

The long struggle for women's suffrage, in both the United States and Europe (it was granted first in New Zealand, in 1893), united women across class and race in a way that earlier campaigns, for example on women's education, had not. But it suffered the common fate of single-issue politics: the movement largely disintegrated once the vote was won, and it was even further undermined by the failure of politically empowered women to change the world in which they lived.

Renewed philosophical impetus came in the 1950s, most importantly from the French existentialist philosopher Simone de Beauvoir. Her insight that woman was entirely defined by her relationship to man was particularly telling in a decade where women had given their wartime jobs back to men and returned to domesticity in greater numbers than ever.

Second-wave feminism, the women's liberation movement, was very specifically a grassroots movement, an aspect of the 'new left' of the 1960s. Although its most articulate theorists, radical figures of the left like Kate Millet and Germaine Greer, rejected conventional politics to encourage an individual understanding of the social constructs that oppressed them, second-wave feminists also identified limited political objectives that would achieve practical advances.

Pragmatic – political – feminism has won some major advances, for contraception and abortion and for improved justice for women victims of violence and rape (including the recognition of rape as a war crime). But some women believe that winning these advances has also proved that sectional interest can damage wider interests. The campaign for equal pay was a political victory but nowhere has it been achieved in practice. A minimum wage has been a more effective way of lifting women out of poverty.

Other feminist political ambitions – equal representation, for example – have only been achieved by the introduction of quotas and distortions of free electoral processes, thus undermining other principles, even including equality. And although, according to the UN, women form 51 per cent of the world's population, do 66 per cent of the work, receive 10 per cent of the income, and own less than 1 per cent of the property, internationally, the limitations of feminism as a political movement have been illustrated by the difficult search for common ground between developed and developing countries.

Still, feminism has a vital influence, if only one among many, on the way that social and political worlds are organised.

Thomas Paine

A brilliant political propagandist more than an original thinker, Paine played a vital role in shaping the American Revolution through the pamphlet 'Common Sense', and the United States Constitution through *The Rights of Man*.

Born: 1737, Norfolk, England
Importance: Pioneered individual liberty, greatly influencing the direction of revolution in the United States
Died: 1809, New York

Thomas Paine left school at 13, antagonised his employers in the Excise Office by demanding higher pay and an end to corruption, and, on the advice of Benjamin Franklin, decided to make his way in America, arriving in 1774. His first pamphlet, 'Common Sense', was published in January 1776. The colonial conflict with England was at a climax and Paine's vibrant justification of the American position, articulating the case for liberty and rallying the troops, sold half a million copies within a few months and paved the way for the signing of the Declaration of Independence on July 4, 1776.

Over the next seven years he wrote a series of 'Crisis' pamphlets to bolster Washington's armies. Later he gave some of his own limited capital to the cause and embarked on a fund-raising tour of Europe to keep the American armies in the field.

In 1789, Paine travelled to England where he read the newly published attack by Edmund Burke on the French Revolution (see pages 30–31). Paine's response, *Rights of Man* (1791), was a radical statement of individual liberty. It made him a wanted man in England – he fled before its publication and never returned – and a hero in France, where he was immediately elected to the National Assembly despite a complete ignorance of French.

Like all the radicals of the 18th century, from Locke (see pages 20–21) to Rousseau (see pages 24–25), Paine found the origin of individual rights in a state of nature in which individuals had enjoyed freedom and had given it up to protect other rights. All government existed exclusively to preserve liberty, property, security and independence: any breach could legitimately be resisted because sovereignty resided in the whole nation and not in any single part of it.

The opening sentences of the US Constitution were strongly influenced by Paine: 'We hold these truths to be self-evident, that all men are created equal, that they are endowed by their Creator with certain unalienable Rights, that among these are Life, Liberty, and the pursuit of Happiness. – That to secure these rights, Governments are instituted among Men, deriving their just powers from the consent of the governed.'

In seeking to show how the sovereignty of the people could end poverty and war, unemployment and illiteracy, Paine proposed a greater role for government – in education, public works and progressive taxes – than many Americans would still accept two hundred years later. But at the time it was his rejection of organised religion, widely misinterpreted as atheism, that destroyed his reputation. His obituary notice declared that 'he had lived long, did some good and much harm'.

> 'These are the times that try men's souls. The summer soldier and the sunshine patriot will, in this crisis, shrink from the service of their country; but he that stands it now, deserves the love and thanks of man and woman.'
>
> Paine ('Common Sense')

Edmund Burke

Edmund Burke was the voice of conservatism and constitutionalism in the face of radical challenge, whose *Reflections on the Revolution in France* prompted Thomas Paine's riposte, *The Rights of Man* (see pages 28–29).

Born: 1729, Dublin, Ireland
Importance: Rejected the idea of radical political change in favour of more organic, evolutionary progess
Died: 1797, Buckinghamshire, England

Burke was born in Dublin, the son of a solicitor. He came to London to study law but abandoned it in favour of the pleasures of Enlightenment London. He started the Annual Register, a survey of world affairs, in 1757, the year he married. In 1765 he became involved in Whig politics.

For much of the 18th century, king and parliament disputed the extent of their power. In *Thoughts on the Cause of the Present Discontents* (1770), Burke defended parliament. He argued that party – previously a term of abuse – could, if organised to advance certain principles, serve as a guarantor of freedom and link between people and executive.

Burke accepted that change was unavoidable and sometimes even desirable, but argued that it should be incremental, based on immediate need rather than metaphysical ideas like individual rights. Change, he argued, should not pursue some moral ideal in opposition to the existing order, thus risking a violent reaction. He dismissed the abstract ideals of liberty and equality and recommended instead the modest ambition of trying to reconcile all the elements of the good life of the whole community.

In 1774, he became bound up in the battle over taxation with America and published *On American Taxation* and, the following year, *On Moving His Resolutions on the Affairs of America*. Declaring his hatred for the colonists' 'metaphysical' rights-based arguments, he defended parliament's right to levy taxes (although he warned parliament that it was wrong to do so because it ignored the mood of the governed and risked provoking justified revolt).

Not surprisingly, he was profoundly opposed to the French Revolution. In his 1790 *Reflections on the Revolution*, he argued against the abstract idea of popular sovereignty contained in the slogan the 'rights of man'. He was dismayed by the complete overturning of tradition and values, and held up as a model England's organic evolution to constitutional monarchy.

> 'A disposition to preserve, and an ability to improve, taken together, would be my standard of a statesman.'
>
> Burke

Burke was also deeply concerned about the state of his native Ireland, where he argued for greater independence, especially from the restrictive economic and religious conditions under which it was governed. But it was the corrupt state of affairs in India that came to dominate his political life. He wanted India governed by an independent commission that excluded both the king and the East India Company. Carried away by his argument, he supported the unjust impeachment in 1794 of Warren Hastings, Governor of Bengal.

Burke doubted man's power to change radically so complex an organism as society. 'We are afraid to put men to live and trade each on his own private stock of reason; because we suspect that this stock in each man is small, and that the individuals would do better to avail themselves of the general bank and capital of nations and of ages.'

Henri de Saint-Simon

Saint-Simon, sometimes seen as the grandfather of socialism, was convinced of the potential of science to transform the political as well as the physical world and argued that society could evolve peaceably into a planned economy managed in the common good.

Born: 1760, Paris, France
Importance: Introduced the idea that a just society could be maintained if well administered
Died: 1825, Paris, France

Henri de Saint-Simon was among the first to try to draw lessons from the revolution in France. He developed a philosophy of history that attempted to explain the evolution of society from medieval to contemporary times, ideas that were later taken up by Karl Marx (see pages 38–39).

Saint-Simon identified the impact of economic development on the organisation of society and the undermining of spiritual and temporal power. The growth of industry, the more cooperative and less coercive nature of industrial leadership, and the rise of science and scientific scepticism weakened the power of the Church and state. The violence of the French Revolution, Saint-Simon believed, came about because the king mistakenly backed the nobility rather than the new industrial classes. But the industrial classes were not fully prepared for their role, and so the monarchy had to be reinstated.

However, this period, dominated by the lawyers and middlemen thrown up by revolution, was only a staging post to a just society where the state, whose function was principally to coerce, would become unnecessary. It would be replaced by administration: 'It is enough for the maintenance of order that matters of common interest should be administered.' In this society, where there was no longer a disparity of wealth that required protection, everyone would understand that the laws were in their interests and would obey them voluntarily.

Above: A primitive feudal society develops through advances in science and industry to a system of perfect justice where all wealth is evenly distributed.

Administrators would be experts, just as scientists are experts, and their expertise would be the management of resources. Saint-Simon saw no reason why ordinary people, without appropriate education, should understand how to administer any more than they understood science. These ideas were elaborated in a series of letters grouped as 'L'Organisateur', addressed either to the king or to the captains of industry whom Saint-Simon thought would, once they understood their role in progress, renounce privilege and step forward to bring about a fraternal society in which each would be rewarded according to his contribution.

Saint-Simon believed a religion was necessary to dictate society's goals and explain the world, but for much of his life he rejected Christianity in favour of science. However, in the year he died, he published his most influential book, *The New Christianity*; Christianity as a system of moral values could, he felt, provide one overriding objective 'to guide the community toward the great aim of improving as quickly as possible the conditions of the poorest class'. It was this idea – supported by practical but radical proposals for tax reform that would prevent the excess accumulation of capital – that his disciples adopted as the creed of the Saint-Simonian religion that spread across Europe for a time after his death.

Auguste Comte

Comte, an early collaborator of Saint-Simon (see pages 32–33), developed philosophical positivism, an attempt to find the rules by which humans could attain happiness. He called his new science of society 'sociology'.

Born: 1798, Montpelier, France
Importance: Developed ideas about sociology that went on to influence generations of scientists
Died: 1857, Paris, France

Auguste Comte rejected both the Catholic faith and the Royalist cause of his parents in favour of an alternative, scientific explanation for the history of human society. He quarrelled with his mentor, Saint-Simon, when the latter rediscovered Christianity, as he later quarrelled with his employers at École Polytechnique, which left him penniless and dependent on admirers such as the English utilitarian John Stuart Mill for funds.

Comte's youth was overshadowed by the aftermath of France's defeat in the Napoleonic Wars. Like many of his contemporaries, he sought a new order that would both replace what the revolution had destroyed and answer the questions that developments in science and industry were raising. Like Saint-Simon, he came to think that science held the answers.

Comte identified three stages of intellectual development: the basis of knowledge passes from the mystical and spiritual to the metaphysical (where explanations are abstract speculation), then to the 'positive' stage, where knowledge is based on empirical observation, limited only by the bounds of human understanding and experience.

Believing that the greater the sum of human knowledge, the smaller the total of human misery, Comte was a man of systems. He categorised the sciences, which he viewed as developing from mathematics and astronomy to physics, chemistry and biology and progressing to his own invention, the science of society, or 'sociology'. Sociology would identify laws by which society was governed in the same way that the natural philosophers had started to map the laws that governed the physical world around them two hundred years earlier. 'From such demonstrations will follow,' he predicted, 'the general or special rules of conduct most in accordance with the universal order, rules which, consequently, will usually be found conducive to individual happiness.'

> 'Men are not allowed to think freely about chemistry and biology: why should they be allowed to think freely about political philosophy?'
>
> Comte

He thought there were two types of sociology: a study of the forces that held society together and a study of the drivers of change. The individual tended to be the latter, the state or government the former. A lot of his thinking was the codification and systemising of Saint-Simon's disorganised genius. Both looked to the structure of the Church, although not its content, for a model of the moral organisation of society, and Comte saw sociologists as the new priests of 'the philosophical foundation of human sociability'.

Much of Comte's political thought was unadventurous and conservative. He rejected democracy and preferred hierarchy and elites. Some of his ideas were plain eccentric: he proposed a new positivist religion with a calendar of positive saints and himself as High Priest. But his ideas about sociology influenced generations to come, including Emile Durkheim in France and Herbert Spencer in England. As the father of sociology, his work remains an important area of study.

Socialism

Despite its ideological origins and a period of dogmatism, socialism has evolved into a broad set of values incorporating fairness and social justice.

Socialism emerged in the 19th century as a reaction to the Industrial Revolution. Industrialisation disrupted communities and traditional work patterns, reduced millions to poverty and brought untold wealth to a few. Its great cities, factories and workshops bred a new kind of solidarity and collective identity, a new trade unionism and, soon, new political theories.

The French utopian socialists like Saint-Simon and Fourier, and the practical reforming Welshman, Robert Owen, all sought an alternative to the private property that appeared at the heart of the injustice of capitalism and an end to the coercive state. The most enduring ideas came from Owen, a successful capitalist himself, who experimented with cooperative production, attacked waste and promoted education.

It was in the hands of Karl Marx and Friedrich Engels (see pages 38–39) that the ideas of socialism became a coherent international doctrine. In capitalist society, where ownership is concentrated in ever fewer hands, the alienated proletariat would one day revolt, capture the means of production and establish a classless society. Socialism would be the final stage before the withering away of the state.

This idea, outlined in the *Communist Manifesto* (1848), shaped European social democracy. But at the outbreak of war in 1914, most socialist parties abandoned the internationalism that had been an integral part of the movement to join the war effort. The communist revolution in Russia in 1917 led to the final split on the left. Moderate socialists were attacked by Lenin for collaborating with the imperialist warmongers, and in turn attacked the new Soviet dictatorship for its failure to return power to the workers.

But despite the failure of the international movement, Soviet communism's apparent economic successes greatly impressed socialists everywhere. In government, however, socialism's early steps in power were tentative and disastrously constrained by world economic crisis. In Germany, the social democrats responded to the depression that followed the financial crash of 1929 with orthodox deflation, as did the minority British Labour government in the same period. Only in Sweden did a social democrat government respond with public works that cut unemployment and reinvigorated the economy.

After the Second World War, socialism became the dominant European ideology, stripped of any reference to revolutionary change. In Britain, although Labour's constitutional commitment to public ownership remained until the 1990s, the first majority Labour government only nationalised a handful of industries and did so in a centralised and bureaucratic manner that contributed to their eventual failure. Its last success was a social revolution that brought universal access to free health care and education, hugely extended welfare benefits, and guaranteed full employment.

Socialism came to mean welfarism, gradualism and mixed economies, and in that modest form enjoyed a period of electoral success across Europe in the 1950s and 1960s. It was adopted in name (although rarely in fact) in many of the newly independent countries of Africa and Asia.

By the late 20th century it was widely accepted that socialism had to change again. Increasingly it has come to represent a movement for the good society – fair, meritocratic, inclusive – within a capitalist economy.

Karl Marx and Friedrich Engels

Marx and Engels, philosophers and propagandists, founded the revolutionary tradition and popularised historical materialism: all history was the history of class struggle and class was a product of economic status. Thus the revolutionary struggle of labour against capital was inevitable.

Born: (Marx) 1818, Trier, Prussia; (Engels) 1820, Barmen, Prussia

Importance: Developed the idea of historical revolutionary change and the inspiration behind the Russian and Chinese Revolutions

Died: (Marx) 1883, London, England; (Engels) 1895, London, England

Marx was the son of a German-Jewish lawyer and fled to Paris after offending the Prussian authorities with his liberal critique of the state of the poor. In 1844, he began the collaboration with Engels – the son of a textile manufacturer – that would influence world politics for the next hundred years.

Marx and Engels worked together developing their materialist concept of history, which argued that the economically dominant class will structure society to promote its own interests: the state was the 'steering committee of capitalist society'. The proletariat was alienated from the labour process. When it became conscious of its alienation, it would be ready for revolution.

Marx and Engels dismissed as 'utopians' the French and British socialists – Saint-Simon and Comte in France (see pages 32–33 and 34–35) and Robert Owen in Britain – and proposed ten immediate steps to communism, which included progressive taxes and compulsory education. The programme opens with the warning 'A spectre is haunting Europe – the spectre of communism,' and ends with the dramatic cry 'Workers of the World, Unite!'

In London, Marx and Engels contemplated the failure of constitutional democracy and decided that in future there must be revolutionary workers' committees alongside bourgeois assemblies that would raise the consciousness of the proletariat. But the pair remained resolutely materialist, denouncing attempts to provoke revolution and insisting it would arrive with economic downturn. Like Saint-Simon, from whom he borrowed heavily, Marx saw revolution as a process by which not just society but humankind itself would be changed. This change would not happen merely by the workers taking power. 'Pure will' could not replace 'actual conditions'.

In 1867, the first volume of *Das Kapital* was published. Here Marx expounded his theory of surplus value: wages are kept at subsistence level by the large pool of unemployed labour. Workers produce more than they are paid for. The employer confiscates the difference – the surplus value. Introducing more sophisticated production methods increases capital outlay and thus reduces profits, and the worker is squeezed to make up the difference.

Marx and Engels made vital contributions in the field of economics and business practice, arguing that social organisms follow an inevitable path of development. At some point, owing to these inescapable economic forces, capitalism would collapse and be replaced by a higher form of society. 'The expropriators [would be] expropriated.'

Proletariat: From the Latin *proles* (meaning 'offspring'), the term describes a class who have no wealth other than their children. Marx extended the term to apply to the working class in general: those who have nothing to sell but their time, who produce goods without owning the means of production. These workers would be the force behind the socialist revolution.

Antonio Gramsci

A leading figure in the early days of the Italian Communist Party, Antonio Gramsci became far more influential as a pioneer of cultural studies and critical theory in the decades after his death than he had been as a Marxist during his short life.

Born: 1891, Ales, Sardinia
Importance: Recognised the need for a working-class voice in the running of the state
Died: 1937, Rome, Italy

Gramsci was initially a socialist but, after the First World War, formed a communist group that took part in Italy's 1921 General Strike. Gramsci spent 18 months in Moscow at the Communist International and returned to lead his party in 1924. But, in 1926, he was arrested and spent the rest of his life in prison or under guard in the hospital.

During his years in prison, Gramsci attempted to formulate a detailed analysis of the conditions that would lead to a successful Marxist revolution. This analysis was published later as *Prison Letters*, although his ideas did not circulate widely until after the Second World War. He developed a new theory of hegemony, a concept Marx and Lenin had used to describe the political leadership of the working class. But Gramsci applied it to culture, explaining how the exchange of ideas across Europe (and later America) from the 17th century onwards had paved the way for Napoléon:

'Each new comedy by Voltaire, each new pamphlet moved like a spark along the lines that were already stretched between state and state, between region and region, and found the same supporters and the same opponents everywhere and at every time. The bayonets of Napoléon's armies found their road already smoothed by an invisible army of books and pamphlets that had swarmed out of Paris from the first half of the 18th century and had prepared both men and institutions for the necessary renewal.'

Capitalism was supported by the prevailing bourgeois cultural hegemony, and Gramsci argued that the working class needed an international culture of its own that would wean it from its current identification with bourgeois values. He saw Christianity as the underpinning of those values, and in particular acknowledged the success with which the Roman Catholic Church held its communicants together regardless of their differing levels of intellecutal attainment, a project he wanted Marxism to emulate.

Gramsci wanted to develop working-class intellectuals who could articulate the working-class experience, and so contribute to the creation of a working-class cultural hegemony. Its significance lay partly in his distinction between civil and political society. Political society, he thought, was the state and the law; civil society included the economy. One was the realm of force, the other of consent, although they self-evidently overlapped. The bourgeoisie, he maintained, kept control over civil society by well-timed concessions to the workers through the political sphere even when those concessions were not in their immediate economic interest. To change this, the workers would first have to win control of, or at least a position in, civil society – although ultimately there might have to be a violent 'war of movement' to capture it. Ultimately, political society would become redundant, as civil society would be able to regulate itself.

John Rawls

The leading political philosopher of the 20th century, John Rawls argued that the first duty of the liberal state was to safeguard individual civil liberties, to allow the right to prevail over the good. His most important work was his *Theory of Justice* (1971). At a time of political extremes, he found what many recognised as a satisfying middle way.

Born: 1921, Baltimore, Maryland
Importance: Among the first politicians to entertain the idea of equal opportunities
Died: 2002, Lexington, Massachusetts,

Rawls was born in Baltimore and worked as an academic at some of the leading US universities, spending the last thirty years of his career at Harvard. As a veteran of the Second World War, and having lived through the Cold War, he was always concerned with the claims of individual liberty within an egalitarian concept of justice against the demands of both Soviet communism and laissez-faire capitalism.

He rejected utilitarianism because it did not guarantee the rights of a minority against the majority. Instead he modernised contract theory. In a group in which each member chooses to ignore his or her origins (class, race or gender), reason and self-interest would lead to two principles. Every person should have the degree of liberty compatible with the liberty of others, and social and economic inequalities should be to the greatest benefit of the least advantaged. A regime of equality of opportunity should prevail. Thus, when the group's origins cease to be ignored, and members find that they are disadvantaged, they will still accept their situation because they can see that it is fair.

Rawls broke with his 18th-century predecessors like Locke by excluding property from the individual liberties that otherwise include all the familiar rights of freedom of thought, conscience and association. Indeed, property could not be one of these liberties, for no right can be infringed even in the interests of welfare or equality, and the second part of his formula, the 'difference principle', might oblige redistribution of wealth in the interests of benefitting the least well off.

Rawls also rejected both Soviet communism, which denied basic liberties, and laissez-faire capitalism because of the injustice of its distribution of wealth, which caused inequality of opportunity. 'The loss of freedom for some,' he argued, could never be 'made right by a greater good shared by others.'

Twenty years after he published his *Theory of Justice*, Rawls modified its arguments to present his ideas as a less philosophical and more narrowly political defence of liberalism, based on reciprocity, respect and fairness, that did not rely on ideas of God or morality. It would offer grounds, he hoped, for 'an overlapping consensus'.

'Ideally citizens are to think of themselves as if they were legislators and ask themselves what statutes, supported by what reasons satisfying the criterion of reciprocity, they would think is most reasonable to enact.'

Rawls

Disappointed by the direction of welfare capitalism and widening income disparities in the 1980s and 1990s, Rawls's final work, *Justice as Fairness: A Restatement* (2001), suggested he now thought only a property-owning democracy or market socialism – two political systems where equality was broadly maintained – could aspire to his kind of egalitarian liberalism.

Conservatism and Neoconservatism

Conservatism and neoconservatism are less closely related than their etymology suggests. Conservatives are pragmatic traditionalists, venerators of established institutions, tolerant of inherited position. Neoconservativism is a 20th-century ideology, a response to the 1960s counterculture in the United States. Its adherents are most identifiable in international affairs as globally hawkish exporters of democracy.

To be a conservative tends to be a state of mind rather than a set of political principles. Conservatives would generally be alarmed at the idea of an ideology. Edmund Burke, writing in the era of 18th-century revolution, was the first to identify and extol the benefits of tradition and settled culture and to warn of the dangers of trying to change either from above (see pages 30–31).

Burke upheld certain principles as well as the defense of the established. In the context of resistance by the American colonies to the Stamp Act, he argued that laws had to observe the temper and customs of those on whom the legislation would fall. If an entire people was in revolt, it was probably the law that was wrong, he observed. Pragmatism, and attention to time and circumstance, was the correct course.

But it was in the context of the French Revolution that he became most eloquent. He deplored the rules-based 'rights of man' not only because it had no organic connection with the culture or experience of France, but also because it set out deliberately to destroy them.

Conservatives regard humans as incapable of perfection. Therefore, government efforts to legislate improvement are a waste of time. The abstract is anathema. Conservative parties are often associated with religious observance – the German Christian Democrats, for example.

There is a corresponding appreciation of constitutionalism and tradition, which in 19th-century Europe was the foundation for a sustained anti-revolutionary alliance that came to be closely associated with nationalist movements.

With the rise of socialism and the decline of liberalism, conservatism absorbed some liberal concerns along with liberal support. Intermittently, it is associated with liberal positions on the 'small' state (government that interferes as little as possible with its citizens) and a strong respect for individual freedoms that once were liberal territory.

Neoconservatism developed as a backlash against higher taxation and greater state intervention of President Lyndon B. Johnson's Great Society initiatives in the 1960s, but most of all in response to a perceived moral crisis – the threat of social chaos and the destruction of moral norms in a society of sex, contraception and abortion.

The search for order to fend off chaos led to its distinctive mission to combat communism. President Ronald Reagan's attack on the 'evil empire' of the Soviet Union was an inspirational moment. It subsequently evolved into a demand that not only should America react, but it should also go out positively to spread democracy and American culture and values. One justification advanced by the 'neocons' is that Western values will trump other, undemocratic, values (in particular extremist Islamic terrorism), which, it is argued, are based on poverty, a lack of economic opportunity and too close an association between religion and state. It is also claimed that democratising the world will spread peace.

Alexander the Great

With a passion for conquest and scientific investigation, Alexander the Great created the first western empire and laid the foundations of the Hellenistic world on which the Roman Empire and, later, the Christian world were built.

Born: 356 BC, Pella, Macedonia
Importance: Creator of the first western empire
Died: 323 BC, Babylon

Alexander the Great inherited the Macedonian throne from his father, Philip II, in 336 BC. Over the following 13 years he brought down the Persian Empire – the greatest superpower of his time – and conquered territory extending from Egypt to India.

Alexander's legacy shows a purpose far beyond the haphazard capture of cities controlling ancient trade routes, or even the revenge and humiliation of a troublesome enemy. He died planning a new campaign that would have brought him mastery of the entire Mediterranean coast, proposing, on his death bed, that 'cities should be merged and slaves and manpower exchanged between Asia and Europe, Europe and Asia in order to bring the greatest two continents to common concord and family friendship by mixed marriages and the ties of kith and kin'. (Although in practice this ambitious boast may have been propaganda to disguise the subordination of his empire to Hellenistic culture.)

Alexander introduced monarchy to the western world. The king became the single source of authority who, in contrast with the tradition of the Greek city-states, now stood at the apex of a pyramid of power. Like Alexander, his successors were required to excel in military leadership. War now became a serious and highly professional undertaking with armies often as many as 80,000 strong. The ruthless demand for obedience imposed by Alexander on his followers was emulated by his successors. He 'franchised'

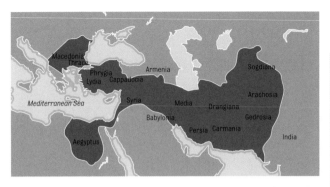

Above: Alexander's legacy was a cultural and political hegemony that crossed continents and remained influential for centuries after his death.

authority to the new cities he left in his wake. Modelled on Greek principles, these cities were ruled by a single governor who extended a cultural as well as an economic hegemony that tolerated little opposition. Alexander was said to have founded 70 cities from Sogdia to Kandahar and back to Egypt, each bearing his name and equipped with gymnasiums, temples, festivals and theatres, all of which were tools to extend and sustain Greek dominance. Although, for example, in Egypt, pre-existing cultural traditions continued, in the bureaucracy through which Alexander's successors ruled, the ability to thrive invariably meant going Greek.

In addition to his military obsession, Alexander interested himself in the causes of the flooding of the Nile, in cataloguing natural history, and in charting his new territories. Greek settlers brought their learning to the east, and opened routes for the passage of eastern ideas to the west. In Egypt, Alexander's successor, Ptolemy, saw a flowering of science and scholarship. Everywhere, Greek became the language of success. Alexander's empire was short lived but his cultural legacy can still be traced.

Shih Huang-ti

The state of Ch'in – which gave its name to China – had been aggressively conquering surrounding states for more than a hundred years before the boy king, Chao Cheng, established the Ch'in Empire in 221 BC. The boy king became *Ch'in Shih Huang Ti*, 'First Sovereign Emperor of Ch'in'.

Born: c.259 BC, Ch'in, China
Importance: Established a centralised state power in China for the first time
Died: 210 BC, Shaqiu, China

Ch'in's success lay in its sophisticated centralised state power. It created a rigid and uniformly applied system of laws, initially within its own boundaries, and later throughout its conquered territories. Divided into 40 prefectures, each was administered by a bureaucracy monitored by a series of officials responsible directly to the central state.

Cultural uniformity was also imposed: the writing system and weights and measures were standardised. Feudal privileges were abolished, highways were constructed to facilitate the movement of troops, and – although this is disputed – all books except those with a direct practical application, such as medicine, were burned in order to halt subversive thought.

The greatest monument to this mighty, but short-lived, dynasty was, for 2,000 years, thought to be the Great Wall, a system of garrisons and signal towers linking some existing fortifications that finally extended from the Bo Hai across Inner Mongolia to Huang He and finally to what is now Gansu province. But Shih Huang-ti was terrified of death and had also constructed a vast burial compound, first uncovered in 1975, in which 6,000 life-size terracotta soldiers had been created to guard his tomb, itself at the heart of a network of palaces.

Shih Huang-ti's construction projects, which entailed conscripting thousands of forced workers, many of whom died on the way, and levying huge taxes, led to unrest. His empire lasted just four years after his death. The emperor had been interested in theories of government and is known to have read and admired the essays of Han Fei, known as

> 'He makes the law measure merits and makes no arbitrary judgment himself.'
>
> Han Fei, contemporary philosopher

the greatest of China's legalist philosophers. He justified breaking with the Confucian past (and the Confucian requirement for virtue in a king) by arguing that historical circumstance required particular forms of government: political institutions naturally reflected differing forms of behaviour, and human behaviour changed depending on external conditions.

As they were living in times of scarcity (possibly brought about by the emperor's tax regime), the people were quarrelsome and needed a king who could impose order: he did not need to try to make men good, only to prevent them doing harm. People were too selfish and infantile to recognise their own true interests, so it was futile for the king to try to win their hearts.

Central to Shih Huang-ti's political stance was his belief that, as long as a king had authority, he had the right to demand obedience, however unworthy he might be deemed. Political fealty was the supreme obligation, above even the soldier's duty to serve his father. He must also pay close attention to the efficiency of his administrators and prevent them exceeding their power or idling on the job. He can trust no one, must prevent anyone gaining more influence than another, and may use cunning to unearth plots against him.

Julius Caesar

Julius Caesar's military and political achievements laid the foundations for an empire that endured for 500 years. He was a leader of genius, a statesman, one of Rome's first historians – and destroyer of the Roman Republic.

Born: 100 BC, Rome, Italy
Importance: Paved the way for a lasting Roman Empire
Died: 44 BC, Rome, Italy

Caesar's career as a military leader was always intended to provide him with the loot and the status to pursue his political ambition: reorganising and rebuilding the Greco-Roman world to secure its stability and prosperity. His inspiration was Alexander the Great (see pages 46–47), and his policies, such as ensuring grants of land for veterans of his armies in the newly conquered territories, focussed on the Romanisation of what was to become the empire.

Caesar formed an alliance with the great military commander Pompey and, by 65 BC, was in charge of, among other things, Rome's games, an opportunity for conspicuous spending in pursuit of public popularity. In 62 BC, he became a magistrate, a rung below the most senior position of consul, but debts forced him to embark on a military expedition in Spain. By 59 BC, he had returned to become one of three consuls running Rome.

In alliance with Pompey and his own financial backer, Crassus, Caesar became governor of Gaul. His successes there during the years from 58–50 BC (which included leading the first attacks on Britain) allowed him to buy influence to further his political ambitions in Rome and shore up his alliance with Pompey, who was accruing power in his absence. By January 49 BC, Pompey had gained control of all Italy's armies. Caesar refused to obey the Senate's command to lay down arms, crossed the Rubicon out of his own territory, and triggered a civil war that, in an extraordinary display of military endurance and leadership, ended in the death of Pompey, the defeat of his supporters in Spain, and the conquest of part of Anatolia and Egypt, where he fell under Cleopatra's spell.

Arguably, in order to rescue Rome from autocracy under Pompey, Caesar had to take the dictatorial powers his enemies had accused him of seeking for his own ends. In the few months in which he exercised these powers, his actions indicate a determination to restore orderly, honest administration. His concerns were with rationalisation: of the calendar, of the laws, of weights and measures. He introduced a standard pattern for the government of Rome's colonies and restored rights to defeated cities like Carthage and Corinth, with the added benefit of providing land for veterans and Rome's rapidly growing urban proletariat. Generous to his defeated opponents (although ruthless in dealing with the 'barbarians' of northern Europe), he extended the right of citizenship to many of the foreigners drawn to Roman colonies. In Rome itself he planned practical initiatives like canalising the Tiber, and he banned wheeled vehicles from the centre of the city.

> 'The evil men do lives after them. The good is oft interred with their bones.'
> Shakespeare, *Julius Caesar*

Caesar used his extensive writing both to promote himself and to justify his cause. Europe's theorists of democracy later condemned his overturning of the last vestiges of popular government in Rome. His success was to create a system of strong government that helped build and preserve the Empire that followed and ensured that his name endures in Western thought 2,000 years later.

Charlemagne

The empire Charlemagne created stretched from northern Spain to the Danube, laying the foundation for a Christian world strong enough to repel the threat of Muslim invasion from the south and from 'barbarians' to the north. Charlemagne's empire survived in name at least for 1,000 years and the idea of its revival has inspired democrats and tyrants ever since.

Born: 747, France
Importance: Created a united Christian Europe
Died: 818, Aachen, Germany

By tradition, Frankish kings relied on military strength to maintain power and Charlemagne was no exception. But there was a new purpose to his warfare beyond shock and awe: the imposition of Christianity. When, after a 30-year campaign, he finally defeated the Saxons, they were converted en masse by the sword. So too were the Friesians and the Slavs to the east of the Danube. He also conquered northern Italy and permanently removed the threat of the Lombards to the Pope.

Creating such a vast kingdom was one thing; the challenge now was to maintain authority across the disparate peoples, customs and languages under his rule. An army of free men, rewarded by land grants in newly conquered territories, and invited annually to an assembly where Charlemagne heard their complaints and they swore fealty, was one weapon. An embryonic bureaucracy, inherited from his predecessors but continually extended and strengthened, was another. Charlemagne also rationalised and standardised weights and measures and used diplomacy to extend trade.

Increasingly the Church bureaucracy became a part of his administrative system. Charlemagne used spiritual authority as a temporal weapon: he and his officials became guardians of the standards and mores of clerics and of ecclesiastical property and

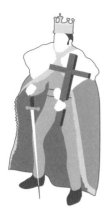

Left: Charlemagne was ingenious in using the trappings of spiritual authority to strengthen his political power.

took control of the appointment of bishops and abbots, hitherto under the auspices of the Church.

Perhaps most importantly, Charlemagne oversaw a cultural 'renewal' too, one that is still visible in the architecture of the churches and the libraries that he created to spread both Christian teaching and the rediscovered works of Greek and Roman times. By reviving texts and disciplines that had almost perished, he provided the basis of the Renaissance.

In 800 CE, Charlemagne went to Rome, where the conduct of Pope Leo III had provoked a revolt. By purging himself, Leo was saved, and, in an act the origins and purpose of which are still debated, crowned Charlemagne emperor, simultaneously giving him the obligation to protect the Pope while lending the power of God to his authority as king.

In 813 Charlemagne crowned his only surviving son, Louis the Pious, Emperor of the Imperium Christianum (the Christian Empire). But the dominance of temporal over spiritual power did not survive his reign. Civil war ensued and, in 1157, by this time exclusively German, it became the Holy Roman Empire.

Genghis Khan

From his origins as a nomadic Mongolian tribesman, Genghis Khan built an empire that, at its most successful, stretched from the Pacific to the Adriatic – the largest contiguous empire in history, whose influence can still be felt in the politics of the region today.

Born: c. 1162, Mongolia
Importance: Used military strategy and fear to build the world's largest contiguous empire
Died: 1227, location unknown

Temujin, as he was initially known, was born into an established tradition of Mongol raiders, although very little about his life can be authenticated. The main source is *The Secret History of the Mongols*, which appears to be largely propaganda.

It is said that Temujin impressed many with his charismatic personality. He emerged at the head of an army of 20,000 with powerful allies and began unifying the Mongolian tribes by dint of massacring their leaders and recruiting their followers into his army. By 1206, through a ruthless pursuit of his objectives regardless of alliance or kinship, he had been proclaimed 'universal ruler', or Genghis Khan.

Having secured his base, Genghis Khan prepared to conquer the peoples on the borders of the new nation. The country itself became an instrument of war, organised to provide and sustain armies, officered by generals chosen for their loyalty. Initially the Mongolian armies consisted of cavalry mounted on the hardy native pony, ideal for swift raids and the removal of plunder. But as he came into contact with more sophisticated enemies, Genghis Khan swiftly developed more sophisticated siege weapons.

He possibly also became literate: it was at this time that the Mongol language was first written down. Or perhaps he simply became aware of the uses of literacy, and learned from his advisers an alternative to plunder as a source of income – taxation on trade, agriculture, and the craftsmen and producers of the conquered territories.

In 1215, following a four-year campaign, Genghis Khan captured Beijing before heading west and south to the Khwarezm Empire in what is now Iran. In revenge for the murder of some traders under his protection, he launched a campaign of exceptional brutality, where his troops ruthlessly massacred whole towns and destroyed gardens and irrigation works. The empire was expanded and consolidated over the next hundred years. Ultimately it stretched across the whole of China while, in Eastern Europe, the challenges posed by the so-called Golden Horde influenced the political development of Russia.

Genghis Khan's extraordinary success was due both to military skill and organisation and to the devastating use of terror that led whole cities to capitulate rather than fight. His armies were known to have developed effective communications, including the use of homing pigeons, which enabled the empire to be held together from the centre. It became increasingly involved in regional trade.

Genghis Khan has become modern Mongolia's greatest hero; he was a figure of resistance during the Soviet era and has become a symbol of national regeneration since.

> 'Possessed of dedicated energy, discernment, genius, and understanding, awe-striking, a butcher, just, resolute, an overthrower of enemies, intrepid, sanguinary, and cruel.'
>
> Minhaj al-Siraj Juzjani, contemporary chronicler

Saladin

Saladin recaptured Jerusalem and much of Arabia from the Crusader kings and made it the base of the short-lived Ayyubid dynasty. He was a devout Muslim and passionate jihadist, renowned for his chivalry in war, his mercy in victory and his generosity to his people, which, it was claimed, upon his death left too little to pay for his funeral.

Born: 1137, Tikrit, Iraq
Importance: Restored Jerusalem to the Muslim faith following capture by the Crusader kings.
Died: 1193, Damascus, Syria

Saladin – also Salah al-Din Usuf ibn Ayyub – was a Kurd whose father migrated to Aleppo in what is now Syria. Aleppo was just beyond the eastern boundary of the disputed Crusader territory that ran along the Mediterranean coast of Arabia and, as a young man, Saladin learned his military skills fighting the Christians.

Nureddin, ruler of Syria and an effective warrior, who had mobilised the local people to help in the jihad against the Christian invader, helped his protégé Saladin claim the throne of Egypt in 1171. Saladin began astutely by wooing the majority of Egyptians, neutralising the Shiite standing army by restoring the Sunni faith. He set about restoring stability and the economy of a country that, for 200 years, had lacked strong rulers.

Saladin was developing into a rival of Nureddin and used the Crusader state as a buffer between himself and Syria. But on Nureddin's death in 1174, Saladin, financed by Egypt's agricultural wealth, marched on Damascus (initially in the name of Nureddin's young son). There he was welcomed, but soon afterward, while unsuccessfully besieging Aleppo, a leader of the Syrian group the Assassins came close to murdering him.

The war against the Christians was prosecuted intermittently. Saladin's first objective was to secure the Muslim territories in what is now northern Iraq and Palestine, as well as in Egypt. Muslims, bitterly divided for most of the 500 years since Muhammad's death and devoid of the zeal that had once taken them to such strength, were attracted to Saladin's evident religiosity, his lack of desire for personal glory and his generosity as a ruler.

In 1187, at Hattin in northern Palestine, he scored a great victory over the armies of the second Crusade. He subsequently had many of his Christian prisoners beheaded. He failed to take Tyre but his forces captured most of the cities along the Mediterranean coast and three months later recaptured Jerusalem, 88 years after it had fallen to the Crusaders. The capture of Jerusalem triggered the Third Crusade, led by Richard the Lionheart who battled with Saladin in an atmosphere of great mutual esteem (Richard at one stage proposing a dynastic marriage between his own sister and

> 'To free the earth of anyone who does not believe in God, or die in the attempt.'
>
> Saladin, recorded by Baha ad-Din

Saladin's son). Among the chivalrous gestures recorded was Saladin's gift of two horses after Richard's had been killed, as well as presents of fruit and the services of his own physician when Richard fell ill.

Like Charlemagne before him (see pages 52–53), Saladin was able to use the trappings of religion to strengthen his political power; but unlike Charlemagne, Saladin used that power in a religious cause. His motivation in taking on the Crusaders appears to have been to spread Muslim religion and practice. Everywhere in his wake he left mosques and colleges and new books promoting jihad.

Ferdinand and Isabella

Ferdinand II of Aragon and Isabella I of Castile united, by their marriage, the two kingdoms of Spain, a unity bolstered by an aggressive Catholicism. This, together with their sponsoring of Christopher Columbus's New World voyages, led to the granting by the Pope of the privileged title of *Reyes Catolicos*, or the Catholic Monarchs.

Born: (Ferdinand) 1452, Aragon, Spain; (Isabella) 1451, Castile, Spain
Importance: United Spain under a single crown for the first time in 700 years
Died: (Ferdinand) 1516, Madrigalejo, Spain; (Isabella), 1504, Medina del Campo, Spain

Spain had been devastated by long periods of civil war and, for Ferdinand and Isabella, establishing their claims to their thrones was an early preoccupation of the marriage. Military glory was one means of promoting their leadership and of occupying potentially troublesome nobles, and the campaign that Ferdinand led against Moorish Granada had the further advantage of cementing Catholics against Muslims.

Initially Ferdinand and Isabella pursued the traditional practice of allowing Moors religious freedom. A fifth of the population of the kingdom of Aragon was still Muslim, and nearly a third were official converts to Catholicism who often continued privately to follow their old religion. Isabella, however, decided on forced mass conversions, and Catholicism was transformed into the weapon most often used to shore up the monarchs' position at home and to justify their expansionist policy overseas.

The Inquisition, a court to ensure true conversion among the non-Christian populace, was set up, as a royal rather than ecclesiastical court with no appeal to Rome – the first of a series of power-grabs by the Catholic monarchs that turned the Church into their tool. Its arbitrary operation in the interests of the king and the terror it inspired became a byword for the abuse of power, familiar by repute to Machiavelli (see pages 12–13) who, in *The Prince*, refers repeatedly to Ferdinand as an exemplar of an effective monarch.

However, unlike Charlemagne and Saladin (see pages 52–53 and 56–57), Ferdinand and Isabella's attempts to use religious power for political gain were not always successful. The first Inquisitor General, Torquemada, prompted the expulsion of the Jews in 1492, effectively stripping out what existed of an urban, educated and skilled middle class in Spain, though providing a valuable source of income through confiscation. At the same time, although Ferdinand and Isabella successfully contained and apparently neutralised the formerly powerful nobility of Castile as they modernised the administration of the state, they left their economic holdings intact. These two factors damaged Spain's potential to develop its economy in the face of growing competition across Europe.

It was not economic development but Christopher Columbus's voyages of exploration to the New World that were to sustain the state. The first of these great journeys, intended by Columbus to find a sea route to the east, was sponsored by Ferdinand and Isabella in 1492. Of all their political machinations, their doctrine of exploration and conquest made their nation rich and formed their lasting legacy in the modern world.

Expansionism:
Doctrine whereby a nation attempts to expand its territorial base, usually by means of military aggression. The discovery of the New World made the acquisition of new wealth and territory fiercely competitive. Modern expansionism often takes the form of manipulation of markets to expand a nation's economic power base.

Colonialism

Colonialism is the imposition by one nation of its sovereignty on another and the consequent subjugation or displacement of the indigenous people.

For most of its history, the motive for colonialism has been to promote and facilitate trade. Secondary reasons have included the suppression of piracy or a hostile country, or simply to prevent a rival power gaining a foothold. Fleetingly in the 19th century, it was held to have a moral purpose – spreading what was deemed to be the superior culture of the west to the primitive peoples of the south.

From the earliest times, colonisation has meant supplanting the indigenous culture with that of the colonisers. This could mean replacing existing administrative systems with structures deemed more sophisticated, raising taxes and enforcing peace.

In the early 19th century, after 200 years of mercantilism, where colonialism had meant the search for a monopoly of raw materials and markets and heavy protective duties, Britain's industrial development made free trade desirable and triggered a new era of colonialism—imperialism. Free trade was more competitive and demanded greater sophistication of supply and ever more profitable markets. Colonial development became more intensive and government became more closely involved.

At the same time there was a vast escalation of migration from Europe to the New World. Between 1820 and 1920, some 55 million Europeans migrated, fleeing poverty and persecution, in search of freedom and prosperity, while the United States saw the great internal migration and colonisation from east to west.

Subjugation of indigenous peoples was made easier by the technology gap: European and American guns were ill-matched against the bows and arrows of indigenous peoples. Where subjugation was impossible or inconvenient, indigenous peoples were often confined to reservations.

Elsewhere, in India for example, a cooperative elite was cultivated, encouraged to absorb western culture and cowed by continued displays of arms. By the late 19th century and into the 20th, ethnographers and social Darwinians were claiming scientific support for the superiority of western races.

Liberal and radical critics began to examine the economic motivation for the race for a place in the sun. In 1902, in *Imperialism, a Study,* J. A. Hobson argued that imperialism was the result of malfunctioning markets. Capitalism was the 'economic taproot' of an imperialism that was otherwise economically neutral at best.

Hobson, a progressive liberal and advocate of social reform, interpreted the rush for colonies as a response to too small a domestic market and lack of competition in industry. Lenin, writing in 1916, came to a similar conclusion. He thought imperialism was the highest – and final – form of a capitalism that had become monopolistic and dominated by financial capital. It shaped its economic environment and drove imperialist wars to sate its need for markets.

After the First World War, Joseph Schumpeter developed what became the most influential argument of the 20th century: capitalism did best in conditions of peace and free trade. Monopolies and imperialism were its enemies.

The defence of empire, by 1945, had become too costly a task for Europe. The retreat happened with spectacular speed: within a generation barely an imperial bastion remained. Instead 'soft' imperialism, the superpower imperialism of arms, cash and culture, took its place.

Elizabeth I

Queen from 1558 until her death 45 years later, Elizabeth gave her name to Britain's golden age. Her reign was a period of literary genius, economic prosperity, individual heroism and military victory, which heralded the rise of the British Empire.

Born: 1533, London, England
Importance: Defied religious tension and rivalry to the throne to reign for 45 years
Died: 1603, Richmond, England

When Elizabeth, the last of the Tudor dynasty, succeeded her half-sister Mary to the throne, a short and bloody reign seemed likely. Religious tension, rivals to the throne and revolt were all brewing. Yet Elizabeth, educated, fluent in French and Italian, and a politician from the topmost jewel in her headdress to the pointed tips of her toes, outclassed them all.

In politics, she was aided by the Tudor concept of kingship, by which the monarch ruled by divine right within a parliament that was understood (however unrealistically) to represent all her subjects. Parliament could be used to quiet potentially troublesome nobles and landed gentry who were often also responsible for maintaining dignity, law and order throughout the land. Economic and social life was strictly regulated. The purpose of the state was to provide a setting not for prosperity but for salvation of the soul.

At home Elizabeth began with the restoration of a degree of religious tolerance ('I shall not make windows into other men's souls') and a settlement that made concessions to Catholics and Protestants. But enough of both remained sufficiently dissatisfied to destabilise her reign both at its start and its conclusion. Catholics repeatedly challenged Elizabeth's legitimacy and advanced the claims of Elizabeth's cousin, Mary Queen of Scots. After several plots (the last of which may well have been exaggerated) Mary was executed in February 1587.

Mary's death, coupled with Elizabeth's provocative support of the Protestant rebellion against Spanish rule in the Netherlands, as well as the often piratical exploits of Elizabeth's two naval heroes, Sir Francis Drake and John Hawkins, was the final trigger for a war with Spain. Philip II of Spain prepared his invasion fleet of 130 great galleons; the English fleet consisted of 200 smaller, more mobile ships. With the help of an Atlantic storm, the Spanish Armada was defeated.

> 'I know I have the body of a weak and feeble woman, but I have the heart and stomach of a king, and of a king of England too.'
>
> Elizabeth I

Elizabeth, rallying her country against the invaders, exploited the moment with a flare for political drama that served her well. She journeyed in the white dress and armour of the Virgin Queen to address troops gathered at Tilbury. 'I know I have the body of a weak and feeble woman,' Elizabeth declared, 'but I have the heart and stomach of a king, and of a king of England too.'

England's overseas exploits – the restless search for plunder, trade routes and new land to claim – laid the foundations of what 300 years later would mature into an empire. The East India Company was founded and so were the first British colonies in North America. But the seeds of 17th-century crisis were also there: the growing importance of parliament, the beginnings of the development of an urban middle class, and the challenge to the idea of rule by divine right. It is perhaps because of the century of turmoil that followed that history remembers Elizabeth as the Gloriana depicted by her contemporary literary admirers.

Akbar the Great

Greatest of the Mogul emperors of northern India, Akbar the Great implemented an enduring administration notable for its religious tolerance in a period when monolithic religious states were the norm.

Born: 1542, Umarkot, India
Importance: Established an administrative structure that lasted over 200 years
Died: 1605, Agra, India

Akbar traced his ancestry back to both Genghis Khan and the notorious conqueror of Persia and Egypt, Timor (or Tamerlane). His grandfather had conquered northern India in 1526 but, on Akbar's accession at just 13, after his father's death (reputedly not in battle but falling from his library steps), most of the gains had been lost. Consequently his reign was dominated by warfare. Unlike his ancestors, however, he treated the defeated Hindu rajas with generosity and honour, as long as they recognised his sovereignty.

A Shi'a Muslim, Akbar's approach to government was strongly influenced by the belief that he was the Imam, the just ruler and recipient of God's divine light, not unlike Plato's philosopher-king, who deserved to be obeyed by virtue of his wisdom and learning. However, Akbar's subjects were predominantly Hindu, with significant populations of Jains, Zoroastrians, Jews and Christians. Muslims were in a minority. Pragmatism demanded a system that acknowledged difference and promoted tolerance, rather than trying to impose uniformity like the Spanish Inquisition in Catholic Spain (see pages 58–59).

Other Islamic states, fearing the weakening of the faith by contact with other religions, had tried forced conversion. But Akbar was able to find religious justification for a state blind to religious difference. The principle of universal tolerance, or *sulahkul*, could be used in conjunction with the theory of the

Imamate to defend decisions also conducive to temporal peace and prosperity. Akbar abolished taxes specific to non-Muslims. Determined to be a just king, in the Platonic sense, he also rejected slavery and immolation of widows.

Famed for his sumptuous court and his patronage of the arts, Akbar took the task of achieving religious harmony so seriously that, through a series of debates with learned representatives of all religions, he developed his own pantheistic religion. It appeared neither to attract – nor to need – many adherents.

Yet he also regarded himself as a devout Muslim and built what he intended to be an ideal city, Fatehpur Sikri, as an earthly representation of Islam, a site of harmony – it reflected Hindu and European as well as Muslim artistic styles. Unfortunately it had no water and was abandoned soon after his death.

Akbar developed a sophisticated system of patronage, which tied soldiers and administrators directly to his own authority. He introduced provincial governors, later known as *nawabs*, who worked alongside a civil administrator and a record-keeper. So efficient was the administrative structure that Akbar designed for managing his empire, levying taxes while keeping the peace and routing challenges from troublesome sons and servants, that it was to form the basis for the British administration in India more than two hundred years later.

Napoléon Bonaparte

Napoléon Bonaparte, Emperor of France (1804–1815), took his lead from Charlemagne and conveyed the ideals of the French Revolution across Europe. He left in his wake a popular belief in the nation-state that, over the next 150 years, shaped not just Europe but the world. In France, his legacy was a centralised system of administration, law, justice and education that enshrined the liberties of the revolution and largely continues to this day.

Born: 1769, Ajaccio, Corsica
Importance: Established a lasting centralised system of administration in France
Died: 1821, St. Helena

Napoléon was born on the French-occupied island of Corsica. His family was of Italian origin but Napoléon was sent to France for his education. His career at the military academy was undistinguished but he was already reading widely – Voltaire and Rousseau and the Encyclopedists – and publishing writings in support of radical reform of his adopted country. He rose to national prominence as the saviour of the republic when he defeated a royalist revolt in 1795; he swiftly became commander of the Army of the Interior then of the Army of Italy, where his wars of conquest began.

Wherever he went, he introduced the ideals of the revolution, provoking the enmity of conservative regimes. In France he became first consul and – having extended the borders of France to the Rhine, the Alps and the Pyrenees – emperor in 1804. Both moves were approved by plebiscite: the people had spoken.

After a short interval of peace following the 1805 naval defeat at Trafalgar, in 1812 Napoléon marched on Russia. Defeat this time was catastrophic. In 1814 he was exiled to Elba in 1815 he marched back into Paris, only to meet final defeat at Waterloo.

In France, Napoléon transformed the administration of the interior, broadly in accordance with the views of philosophers like

Voltaire and Rousseau (see pages 24–25). What became the *Code Napoléon*, the great reform and codification of law, which still governs France, had been begun in 1790. Promulgated in 1804, it guaranteed individual liberty, the freedoms of speech and conscience, and equality under the law.

Central control was exercised through a system of prefects who ran the individual *départéments*. An independent judiciary, appointed for life, was set up, and a national bank, the Banque de France. In one of the most revolutionary moves, secondary education became a state responsibility, as the *philosophes* of the 18th century had proposed.

Despite his own indifference to religion, Napoléon sponsored the Concordat of 1801, by which post-revolutionary France and the Pope were reconciled. The state became entirely secular (so when he was crowned emperor, at the last moment Napoléon took the crown from the Pope's grasp) freedom of worship was guaranteed and the Pope recognised the expropriation of ecclesiastical property.

'What a novel my life is!'
Napoléon

Napoléon's contribution to the development of the idea of nationalism in Europe was arguably less direct, but the revolution, and the redrawing of national boundaries that followed the revolutionary wars, showed people that the political firmament was much less rigid than it appeared. In the end, the same resistance to domestic rulers was applied to Napoleonic rule too. In Spain, Italy and Germany, national feeling inspired opposition to Napoleonic hegemony and contributed to his ultimate defeat.

Nationalism

Traditionally, nationalist philosophy demands the loyalty of the individual to the nation-state and offers the individual an identity. Nationalism is an exclusive ideology; it defines itself by what it is not as well as by what it is. Continually evolving, the nation-state in the 21st century might be displaced as a centre of loyalty by religion or ethnicity, allowing the unity implied by nationalism to transcend traditional geopolitical boundaries.

The idea of the nation-state was the wedge used to destroy the great, centralised empires of the 19th century – the Habsburg, the Ottoman and ultimately the British. From Roman times, loyalties had tended to be a mix of the parochial and the universal: the feudal baron and the Holy Roman Emperor.

The origins of nationalism can be traced to the English Reformation, when England began to articulate an identity in the context of the virtues of the liberty it had gained through independence from Rome, against what was felt to be the miserable servitude of those still in its thrall. Threats from Catholic Spain in the 16th century encouraged the trend.

In Europe, Napoléon's campaigns in the name of liberty triggered loyalty to an idea that loosened the loyalty to the despotic monarchs he deposed. Subsequently, opposition to Napoléon generated a new sense of territorial, cultural and linguistic loyalty that, when allied to Rousseau's ideas of popular sovereignty and the 'national will', began to develop into the powerful political weapon of the late 19th century.

The creation or discovery of a national identity was a crucial element in the nationalist struggles that ensued. It was often inspired by a romantic rediscovery of ancient custom and literature, campaigns for the reinstatement of a suppressed language and a stress on ethnicity. Religion was often, but not invariably, part of the mix.

After the Treaty of Versailles (1919) had completed the destruction of the European empires by granting nationhood to the states of Eastern Europe, the weaknesses inherent in the nationalist idea set about undermining the peace. Hitler came to power by promising to restore German greatness after its betrayal by its former leaders. Later he exploited German cultural identity to justify both his expansionist territorial ambitions in the Rhineland, Austria and Czechoslovakia, and his racist domestic policies that led to the Holocaust.

But as nationalism was discredited in Europe it achieved success as inspiration to the anti-colonial movement. Territorial nationalism in India's independence movement led to religious nationalism in Muslim Pakistan, which refused to be part of a Hindu-dominated India.

From the anti-colonial movement, nationalism returned to America as an idea behind radical black power movements. Today, religious nationalism is a powerful factor for Muslim minorities around the world.

In an age of global trade, fear of terror and mass migration, Western countries (especially former colonial powers) are looking for ways of articulating a national identity that does not rely on shared history, religion or culture; open to all, it is an echo of America's Pledge of Allegiance – immunisation against the extremism of the outsider.

Catherine the Great

During her reign (1762–1796), Catherine the Great expanded Russia's borders to the Black Sea and into central Europe. She came to the throne as a liberal, a student of Voltaire and Rousseau (see pages 24–25). She died a reactionary, an autocrat whose reforms served only to strengthen her own and her nobles' control over the ordinary people of Russia, and whose expansionary policy increased the likelihood of European conflict.

Born: 1729, Stettin, Prussia
Importance: Ruled Russia for over 30 years and employed a rigorous expansionist policy
Died: 1796, St. Petersburg, Russia

Catherine was the daughter of well-connected but minor German royalty, plucked from obscurity by Elizabeth, daughter of Peter the Great, in order to marry her unpromising son, also Peter. For 18 years Catherine endured the humiliation of a backward, hard-drinking, impotent husband, the laughing stock of the court, while privately educating herself in modern kingship with every intention of ruling in her husband's place.

When Elizabeth died, Peter succeeded but rapidly alienated the court, and Catherine quickly usurped Peter's throne with the support of the army. In the name of reform, Catherine confiscated the property of the Orthodox Church, solving the imperial financial crisis and, by maintaining good relations with the major European powers, preserved peace on her western borders while preparing to make war in the south.

The Ottoman Empire was the barrier to a Russian route to the waters of the Black Sea and the Mediterranean. Victory over the Turks was swiftly followed, in 1775, by victory at home over a Cossack called Pugachov, who attempted to reclaim the throne in the name of Catherine's dead husband. This uprising marked a complete reversal in Catherine's original plan to introduce liberalism to her feudal domain. Her revolutionary proposals for constitutional reform – too hot to be published in France, let alone enacted in Russia – were shelved. Russia's serfs, the raw material of the wealth of the landed aristocracy, were not only kept enslaved, but enslaved under more onerous conditions, while serfdom was actually extended into the Ukraine.

'Power without the trust of the nation is nothing.'
Catherine the Great

Catherine underlined the authority of power with the grandeur of her court. She declared herself the Mother of all the Russias, and used every art and artifice to promote an almost mystical aura about her regime, a piece of propaganda enthusiastically supported by foreign rulers.

But already the shadow of revolution was beginning to spread across Europe. Catherine strongly disapproved of the events of France 1789, and as she rightly anticipated, the demand for reform swiftly spread to Poland. The nation was first repressed and then divided between Russia, Prussia, and Austria.

Like many powerful women since, Catherine was accused of a voracious sexual appetite. Traits that would barely be remarked upon in a male ruler were used to undermine her extraordinary if reactionary record as empress of all the Russias in an era that, for all its cruelty, also saw the burgeoning of Russia's economy and the opening up of its society to the West.

Otto von Bismarck

Bismarck, prime minister of Prussia and Germany's Iron Chancellor, united his country's diverse states by war and diplomacy while suppressing all liberal movements at home, preserving it against the threat of revolution.

Born: 1815, Schönhausen, Prussia
Importance: Unified the states of Germany under Prussian rule.
Died: 1898, Friedrichsruh, Germany

The son of a conservative Prussian 'Junker', or landowner, Bismarck was an undistinguished student who seemed destined to run the family estates until he was drawn into conservative politics at the age of 32. Bismarck – curiously echoing his near contemporary Marx – believed the liberal middle classes who triggered revolutions across Europe in 1848 were looking for economic advantage at the expense of the poorer classes. Unlike Marx, he aimed to preserve a conservative order by meeting the desire of the various classes in society for growth and stability. His experience as a representative in the ruling council of Frankfurt, which governed the confederation of German states, turned him from a Prussian conservative into a German nationalist.

In 1862, he became prime minister of Prussia and slowly began to implement the capture of Germany under Prussian leadership, and the confinement of Austria to its southern, Slav, territories. The new 'north German confederation' was given an almost radical constitution, except that Bismarck intended the enfranchisement of the peasant classes to act as a bulwark against liberalism, with the emperor retaining the right to make his own government. In 1870, war with France (and peace terms that, involving the loss of Alsace-Lorraine, rankled the French until 1918) finally secured the support of the south German states, and 'lesser Germany' – without Austria – was created.

Mainland Europe was now divided into four power blocks: Russia, Austro-Hungary, France and Germany. Bismarck's skilled diplomacy – like that of Clemens Metternich in the Austrian interest a generation earlier – was devoted to maintaining the balance of power and defusing any situation that might trigger conflagration, such as the rapid decline of Turkish power in the Balkans. (It was Bismarck who called the Ottoman Empire the 'sick man of Europe'.)

Domestically, to try to secure a similar balance, he secularised the state and dissolved religious orders. When the balance once more seemed to favour the progressives, he introduced a degree of protection for the economy that aided the conservative landowners against the urban social democrats.

> 'It is not by means of speeches and majority resolutions that the great issues of the day will be decided . . . but by blood and iron.'
>
> Bismarck

His aggressive opposition to the left ('rats . . . to be exterminated'), shared by men of his class across Europe for at least two generations afterwards, was reflected in coarse and intolerant language that arguably damaged the prospects for genuine democratic development. But he also stuck with his original analysis and attempted through welfare reform to create client groups among those who might otherwise support revolution. Measures such as an insurance scheme for pensions and socialised medicine were ahead of their time in Europe.

Adolf Hitler

As the Dictator of Germany between 1933 and 1945, Hitler created the doctrine of National Socialism, which declared the authority of the Führer as the representative of the will of the people, while rejecting the freedom and equality that had marked 19th-century European political development.

Born: 1889, Braunau am Inn, Austria
Importance: Founded National Socialism, promoting the idea of Aryan racial supremacy
Died: 1945, Berlin, Germany

Nazism grew from a variety of late-19th-century ideas, among them a romantic nationalism, the notion of Aryan racial superiority, and the German ideal of leadership, particularly as expressed in the Nietzschean concept of a leader whose will transcended all known rules, an 'Übermensch'. It was also influenced by Darwinian ideas of evolution and struggle, from which came the theory of a superior race under threat. With his associates in the National Socialist Party, of which he became leader in 1920, Hitler put these ideas together with Germany's 19th-century militaristic tradition to articulate a message that – in a country economically and socially depressed by defeat in the First World War – appealed across the political spectrum.

During a period in prison, following an unsuccessful coup against the Bavarian government in 1925, Hitler started to write his statement of political theory, *Mein Kampf*. He wrote that the state is the expression and the guardian of the popular will to which every individual except the leader must be subordinate.

Hitler made plain his ambition to unite all the German-speaking peoples of Europe. By stressing a common identity, he was able to weld together the disparate German states. Like Mussolini in Italy, Hitler presented communist Russia as a threat to the life of the German nation that the whole country must unite to oppose. Communism, in Hitler's lexicon, was almost synonymous with Judaism (although the bankers Hitler blamed for Germany's economic collapse were also attacked for their 'Jewishness'). Hitlerian propaganda created a monster out of the Jewish race, which threatened to weaken and undermine Aryan purity. Jews were described as a race without a homeland and thus a 'parasite' on the German people.

The socialist aspect of Nazism is less familiar than the nationalist. But Hitler espoused causes that would, even 70 years later, be considered radical. Nazism was not just anti-capitalist, it was dismissive of liberal freedoms.

Under Hitler's totalitarian rule, approved by plebiscite in 1934, there was neither space for other parties, nor for dissent of any kind wherever it emanated – including the churches. Everything became subordinate to the will of the nation as expressed through Hitler and Hitlerian propaganda, manifested in mass events like the Nuremburg rallies. Uniformity of outlook was reinforced by a powerful state-police apparatus.

Hitler's programme demanded *Lebensraum* (space) and resources that would allow Germany to be self-sufficient while establishing the master race across Europe and North Africa, an empire as great as Caesar's (see pages 50–51). But his refusal to recognise Europe's existing borders finally provoked France and Britain to arms in 1939 and led ultimately to Hitler's defeat in 1945.

Propaganda: Any attempt to manipulate the perceptions and beliefs of a populace to inspire loyalty to the propagandist. Propaganda is essential to a totalitarian regime, which must maintain the belief amongst the people that the leader's aims are in the nation's best interests. Propaganda often creates scapegoats to bear the brunt of national discontent.

Totalitarianism

In totalitarian regimes, the state controls every aspect of public and private life, often in an arbitrary manner and with extreme repression. At its head sits a dictator, reinforced in power by a cult of personality and control of the media.

Totalitarianism is generally understood to be a 20th-century phenomenon, a particular perversion of the very attributes that make liberal democracy, with its dependence on open information and an educated electorate, a possibility.

Totalitarianism is facilitated through mass communication and the mass literacy of the state – the tools of control and propaganda in every home, as described by George Orwell in his novel *1984* (1948). Hitler and Stalin in the West, Mao and Pol Pot in the East have all exemplified the ruthless cruelty of such regimes, leaving millions of their own citizens dead.

In the early 1920s, Mussolini and his ghost-writer, philosopher Giovanni Gentile, promoted the expression 'totalitarian' to describe the kind of hold the state might be able to gain over its citizens through modern communication.

Totalitarian regimes are differentiated from the merely autocratic not only by degree but also because in autocracy remnants of pluralism often play a part in moderating the autocrat's behavior. It is typical of totalitarian regimes that they destroy all pre-existing institutions (sometimes more than once) and make clients of those – such as the Church or trade unions – that they cannot destroy.

Terror is a particular weapon of totalitarianism. It originates in the absence of a settled and open system of law, ensuring that citizens live in a state of perpetual uncertainty, augmented by show trials of the terrible consequences of being caught in error.

The German-American philosopher Hannah Arendt, in her seminal work *The Origins of Totalitarianism* (1951), said terror obliterated individual spontaneity. She identified totalitarianism's reliance on reducing the world's problems to a single issue or enemy – race for the fascist, class for the communist.

'The disturbing relevance of totalitarian regimes,' she wrote, 'is that the true problems of our time cannot be understood, let alone solved, without the acknowledgment that totalitarianism became this century's curse only because it so terrifyingly took care of its problems.'

Unlike other systems of government where, as Montesquieu argued, the concern is to find the best system of law for its purpose, the purpose of totalitarianism is to make the people fit for the system. Some of Jean-Jacques Rousseau's critics argue that in his idea of 'forcing people to be free', there is a justification of the totalitarian regime but, although out of context it is capable of such an interpretation, it is clearly not what he intended.

Preventing a return of totalitarianism has, since the end of the Second World War, become a major concern of Western foreign policy. The argument that dictators must be stopped before it is too late has been used as a defence for aggression from the Suez in 1956, when Nasser was the target, to Iraq and Saddam Hussein in 2003 (although not against Pol Pot in Kampuchea in the 1970s, when the West tolerated the killing fields because the dictator was opposed to communist Vietnam).

Some commentators regard militant Islam as proto-fascist and warn of its capacity to develop into totalitarianism but that would imply an unlikely readiness to depart from the teachings of the Koran and Sharia law.

Joseph Stalin

Perhaps the greatest mass murderer in history, Joseph Stalin brutally transformed the Soviet Union into a mighty industrial economy that at its height rose to challenge the United States and set the stage for the Cold War.

Born: 1879, Georgia, Russian Empire
Importance: Embarked on a ruthless programme of industrialisation, bringing Russia in line with the United States
Died: 1953, Moscow, USSR

Joseph Stalin, born Joseph Dzhugashvili, was raised in poverty in Georgia, then part of the Russian Empire. As an adult he used his heavily accented Russian and his lack of formal education to disguise a cruelly creative political genius. As Secretary-General of the Communist Party, he accrued tyrannical powers that kept him in control until his death nearly 30 years later.

No formal political theorist, Stalin gave his name to a political system dependent on dictatorial powers, a cult of personality and ruthless persecution of opponents. He duped his opponents through both his astute understanding of the nature of power and his success in creating a powerful, easily understood political message, justified by ruthless zealotry in the name of the quasi-religious cult he created for the dead Lenin.

The defeat of proletarian uprisings in Europe, betraying the promise of the world revolution once so confidently foretold by Marx, prompted a revision of communist theory. Economic transformation was necessary to shore up the revolution, prove that Communism under Stalin worked, and prepare the way in the Soviet Union for the final triumph, the victory of the industrial working class, then still only a minority.

In the name of Marxist theology and 'socialism in one country', Stalin created a vast state apparatus charged with bringing about crash industrialisation. The human cost was

Left: Stalinism envisioned a constant battle by the Soviet faithful against capitalist infiltrators, watched over by the revered leader.

terrible but Stalin understood the uses of terror better even than Machiavelli (see pages 12–13). In the name of improving agricultural output and industrialising production, Russia's 25 million peasants were forced onto collective farms. All who resisted were accused of seeking profit by exploiting others. They were either shot or sent to concentration camps. Where one of the new factories failed to achieve its ambitious objectives, its managers were subjected to show trials and executed or internally exiled.

During his second decade in power, Stalin developed the theory of the aggravation of the class struggle. He argued that as the old exploiters faced elimination they would briefly become more dangerous. The 'enemy within' had to be defeated and he expanded the terror to include former political allies and military leaders who were convicted on the basis of fabricated confessions, along with academics and artists.

By relentlessly identifying himself as the defender of his people, Stalin was able to present critics and rivals, and ultimately anyone whom he imagined might one day be either, not just as his enemies but as enemies of the country. Linked with a cult of personality, Stalin's state communism became the method of choice for emerging powers, in particular Mao Tse-tung in China and Kim Il Sung in North Korea.

Empire Builders, Conquerors and Rulers

Simón Bolívar

Simón Bolívar was the first freedom fighter, the 'Liberator' who, in the name of democracy, freed almost one third of South America from Spanish rule and adapted European political theory to Latin American culture.

Born: 1783, Caracas, Venezuela
Importance: A revolutionary leader, liberating much of South America from Spanish rule
Died: 1830, Santa Marta, Colombia

Bolívar was the son of a wealthy Caracas family who sent him to Europe to study. It was here that he came into contact with the ideas of Voltaire, Montesquieu and Rousseau as well as earlier writers like Locke and Hobbes. In legend, he had a blinding flash of his destiny while on a visit to Rome: 'On my honor, I swear not to rest until I have liberated America from her tyrants.' His conversion coincided with the undermining of Spanish authority by Napoléon's invasion of the Iberian peninsula.

Bolívar stands out as an original thinker at a time when the ideas of nationalism and nation-states were beginning to take hold in Europe. He adapted considerations of cultural identity, language and natural frontiers to the realities of South America, where the majority population was indigenous and only a minority Spanish by either race or language.

He envisaged the Americas as a single entity, an idea he developed in his address *To an Inhabitant of Jamaica*. (He had fled to Jamaica following the first of several defeats at the hands of the Spaniards in Venezuela.) He sought what he admitted was a grandiose idea, 'a single nation of the New World', united by race, language, religion and customs.

Inspired by his vision, he led a tiny band of men in a series of extraordinary military victories. Bolívar hoped for a New World order, an Andean empire united under a strong government that would transcend colour and creed, with a common army and navy, in friendship with the liberal regimes of America and Britain.

Bolívar was the prototype 19th-century revolutionary, a military commander of great courage and flamboyant initiative, a charismatic leader and legendary lover. His cry was for independence from Spain, self-government rather than cultural nationalism, and constitutionalism and freedom within boundaries shaped as much by military requirements as any sense of national identity. Struggling with the question of authority versus liberty, he became a convinced supporter of strong government – an early political tract, *El Manifesto de Cartagena*, attributed the collapse of the first Venezuelan republic to a lack of a strong centre. Subsequently, wherever he conquered the Spanish he would, while proposing liberal constitutions modelled on those in Britain, establish himself as dictator.

He was particularly persuaded of the need for a president for life, capable of strong and unchallenged rule. By the end of 1824, he had become president of Gran Colombia and dictator of Peru. Upper Peru become Bolivia in recognition of his achievements.

His final years were clouded by the disintegration of his empire into fratricidal civil war between its component parts. However, the name Simón Bolívar remains a potent symbol of radical nationalism.

Nation-state: A sovereign – i.e. self-ruled – territory comprising and ruled by a single cultural or ethnic group. Imperialism precludes the existence of a nation-state in conquered countries, since political power rests with the colonising nation. Nationalism seeks to restore independent rule, often by promoting indigenous culture.

Giuseppe Garibaldi

In the year of Giuseppe Garibaldi's birth, Italy was dismissed as a 'geographical expression'. By the time of his death, it was a united country with a liberal constitution, a model for nationalist movements throughout the world.

Born: 1807 Nice, France
Importance: Personified the nationalist ideal, becoming the populist inspiration for Italian unification
Died: 1882, Caprera, Italy

The unification of Italy was inspired by the ideas of the *risorgimento*, the rebirth of the nation as a country free of the imperial ambitions of Austria and France, and infused with a moral and spiritual perspective. The soul of Italy was identified with Christianity, but not the Catholic Church. Even monarchy was considered a foreign import.

The *risorgimento* also inspired ideas of personal sacrifice and heroism that were particularly appealing to the soldier Garibaldi, whose dashing conduct in battle became an integral part of the glamour of the new ideology of nationalism. Garibaldi, whose military genius far outshone his intellectual endeavours, was strongly influenced by his contemporary political ally, the republican nationalist and philosopher Giuseppe Mazzini, who was the first to grasp the propaganda value of Garibaldi's exploits in battle. But Garibaldi was also seduced by the appeal of the early socialists, in particular Saint-Simon (see pages 32–33).

In 1834, Garibaldi was exiled to South America, where the exploits of the 'Liberator', Simón Bolívar, were still vivid. Here he learned the techniques of guerrilla warfare before returning to Europe a hero in time for the year of revolutions, 1848.

Having forced the Pope out of Rome, Garibaldi was in turn forced to retreat by a besieging French army. However, in what became one of the great legends of the 19th century, he and a few hundred men escaped from the city and, in a dramatic forced march, reached safety in San Marino. Garibaldi repeatedly showed great personal courage and a willingness to sacrifice himself for his cause – heady propaganda for nationalists around the world. 'Rome or die' was his catchphrase, which he was quick to impress on the dozens of reporters who accompanied him on his campaigns.

> 'This people is its own master. It wishes to be the brother of other peoples, but to look on the insolent with a proud glance, not to grovel before them imploring its own freedom.'
>
> Giuseppe Garibaldi, speech 1860

A further period of exile ended with a renewed vigour for the cause of unification in 1859. By September 1860, in a breathtaking military campaign, Garibaldi and his Red Shirts had captured the kingdoms of Sicily and Naples. These conquests were handed over to Victor Emmanuel, the first king of Italy – a sacrifice that guaranteed Garibaldi world-hero status. Wherever he travelled he was greeted almost as a Messiah: he even baptised children. Lincoln tried to woo him to America to fight in the Civil War but Garibaldi found him unsound on slavery. Instead he pursued further campaigns to liberate Rome from the Pope and to defeat the Austrian Empire, his charisma disguising his occasional lack of military finesse. For more than a hundred years after his death, he remained the quintessential revolutionary figure, as much an inspiration to the dictators of the 20th century as he had been to 19th-century romantics.

Sun Yat-sen

Known as the 'Father of the Republic', Sun Yat-sen led the revolt against the imperial Qing dynasty and, with his original ideas for reform, paved the way for the communist revolution a generation after his death.

Born: 1866, Guangdong province, China
Importance: Applied Western ideas of nationalism, democracy and socialism to Chinese traditions
Died: 1925, Beijing, China

Sun Yat-sen, son of a farmer from southeast China, was educated in a Church of England school in Honolulu and, later, in Hong Kong. He became a Christian, and throughout his life – much of it spent in exile – travelled extensively, gaining familiarity with Western ideas and political developments.

By the late 19th century, the Qing dynasty was in terminal decline, particularly after China's defeat by Japan in 1894. Sun Yat-sen launched several – perhaps as many as 11 – attempted revolutions with little coherent idea at first of what should replace 300 years of authoritarian rule. In 1905, after years in exile in Japan, Europe and the United States, he had developed sweeping proposals for reform. His 'Three Principles of the People' were a synthesis of Western ideas about nationalism, democracy and socialism adapted to Chinese traditions. He saw his mission in terms of a moral and economic crusade, a rebirth for China liberated from the yoke of the emperors and foreigners, reminiscent of the Italian *risorgimento* (see page 82).

His proposals gave central government a powerful role in controlling both the rampant capitalism of the new industrialists and the more traditional powers of the rural landlords. However, he felt the mass of the Chinese people were not ready for democracy. Instead he proposed three periods of 'tutelage', the 'Three Stages of the Revolution', during which the idea of taking

responsibility for government would be gradually introduced and the near-dictatorial powers of the centre would be devolved.

Sun Yat-sen built a revolutionary organisation that, when the Qing dynasty finally collapsed in 1911, he transformed into the Kuomintang, or Nationalist Party. In 1913, the party won a majority of the seats in the new parliament. However, democracy was not well enough entrenched to control military or financial interests and, despite popular support, he was exiled again.

Returning in 1916, Sun Yat-sen began to rebuild support. In the early 1920s, he found new friends among the Chinese Communist Party who persuaded him that embracing communist members would allow his party to reach the millions of peasants and industrial workers still unfamiliar with political organisation. In return, the Soviet Union supplied military and technical advice and arms.

Before he could launch his next coup attempt, Sun Yat-sen died. However, aided by his patron's posthumous glory, his successor, Chiang Kai-shek, finally accomplished the revolution and reunification of China in 1928.

The Bolshevik

Vladimir Ilyich Lenin

Lenin, first of the 20th-century tyrants, engineered the Russian
Revolution of October 1917, led the new Union of Soviet Socialist
Republics through civil war and established the authoritarian
character of a regime that endured for more than 70 years.

Born: 1870, Simbirsk, Russia
Importance: Played a pivotal
role in the Russian
Revolution of 1917, bringing
an end to Tsarist Russia
Died: 1924, Gorki, USSR

Vladimir Ilyich Ulyanov adopted the name Lenin in
1901. A brilliant lawyer, he devoted his life to
revolutionary politics, in particular to developing a
philosophy that would justify Marxist revolution in
Tsarist Russia, a country whose economy was more
feudal than capitalist and therefore unready, in the
terms of *Das Kapital*, for revolution (see pages 38–39).

Lenin argued that, for all the importance Marx
placed on the means of production, they were only
part of a bigger story. Although Russia was no
bourgeois capitalist democracy, the exploitation of peasant
workers in the growing industrial sector created the same
conditions that made western Europe ripe for revolution.

In his 1902 pamphlet 'What Is to Be Done?' Lenin envisaged a
small, militant party that would serve as the 'vanguard of the
proletariat'. It would lead the revolution, rather than wait for it to
happen. It would be run on democratic centralist principles – that
is, under total central control of a revolutionary elite.

In the years before the First World War, strikes and socialist
activity in Britain encouraged Lenin to believe that industrial
Europe was on the brink of revolution, and he developed the
theory that revolution abroad would allow Russia to skip Marx's
ordained period of socialism and move straight to communism.
With the advent of the First World War, Lenin was disappointed
to discover that most socialists supported their country's war

effort. As the world grew war-weary, he declared that revolution was the sole means of achieving a just and democratic peace. In a sweeping condemnation of imperialism that became the primer for anti-colonial uprisings over the next 50 years, he argued that the final stage of capitalism was always the destruction of peace in the search for ever-greater profits.

Returning to Russia after the first revolution of 1917, Lenin adapted his ideas once again. Faced with a liberal constituent assembly, he declared it incapable of delivering peace. Power resided in the soviets, the worker-controlled organisations. The soviets would be the instrument by which state power was destroyed; direct rule by the proletariat would ultimately lead to Marx's utopia where state power withered away. He toppled the first revolution and replaced it with Soviet government.

Lenin believed revolution in Russia would trigger revolution in Europe. But by 1921, Soviet Russia, after three years of civil war, was in economic meltdown. Nimble as ever, Lenin launched the New Economic Policy, a kind of surrogate capitalism, to revive the economy until world revolution came to its aid. There are signs in his *Testament*, written only a year before he died, that he would have made further changes to the party organisation and that he was reflecting on the excessive power that colleagues like Stalin had accrued. But the regime he left, with its implicit belief that social engineering could change human nature, was the regime he had created.

One-party state:
Political system in which only one political party is permitted to form a government or field candidates for election. It is often associated with revolutionary governments, in which the party behind the revolution seizes power. Centralisation of power is intended to prevent the resurgence of the deposed government.

Communism

Communism envisages a political system in which, through the common ownership of the means of production, mankind lives in classless harmony, free from a coercive state. Although there were pre-Marxist experiments in communist living, distinguished by a disavowal of private property, communism as a major political movement was defined by Marx and Engels (see pages 38–39).

Fundamental to their ideas was a communist revolution that would capture power from the bourgeoisie (merchant classes). Such a revolution would arise spontaneously as economic power concentrated into ever fewer hands and the proletariat grew correspondingly more numerous. This would initiate the rule of the proletariat from which communism would emerge and spread across the globe.

Lenin fused Marxism with the Russian tradition of a highly centralised, disciplined revolutionary party, a structure he called 'democratic centralism'. By 1921, with revolution within Soviet boundaries secure, the Communist Party (Comintern) was established on Leninist lines to promote revolution around the world. But if its organisation and ultimate objectives were rigid, its policies were ever-evolving. Bewildered Marxists outside the Soviet Union struggled to keep up with the conflicting edicts emanating from the Comintern. The only consistent message was the monolithic nature of the party. Dissent meant expulsion.

After the Second World War, communism and Stalin achieved an international prestige that gave socialist parties electoral strength in Europe, and communist regimes were established in a belt along the Soviet Union's western border. And at last, in 1949, there was a major revolution in Asia, when the Chinese People's Republic was established.

But the monolithic edifice of Soviet communism was eventually undermined. Marshal Tito's Communist Party in Yugoslavia had a genuine popular base after its role in resistance during the Second World War. When Tito argued that communism could be achieved without revolution and that a world dominated by two superpowers was a threat to peace in itself, Moscow was unable to silence him.

China, under Mao, defended the Stalinist legacy, broke with the USSR under Khrushchev and increased the fragmentation of the single Marxist-Leninist world view. A third challenge to the communist monolith came from the un-Marxist enthusiasm for communism and its message of rapid modernisation among some developing countries. A new, 'non-capitalist' path of development was indicated.

Khrushchev's death was followed by Brezhnev's long freeze and the repression of Czechoslovakian, and then Polish, attempts at liberalisation. By the time Mikhail Gorbachev came to power, the Soviet communist economic experiment was in meltdown and the East European satellites in turmoil.

Gorbachev's reforms were incapable of preventing the final collapse of Soviet communism. In China, too, major reform was underway. After 1991 private enterprise was deemed to be an 'important component' of the socialist economy. The principle of rule by law was accepted. Maoist communism remains strong in Asia in the 21st century but only Cuba remains nominally committed to Soviet communism.

Kemal Atatürk

Atatürk, the first president of the Republic of Turkey (1923–1938), was an ambitious moderniser who defined the modern secular republic, inspiring many imitators and bringing Turkey into the 20th century.

Born: 1881, Salonika, Greece
Importance: Creator of the modern Turkish state – a secular republic
Died: 1938, Istanbul, Turkey

Kemal Atatürk was a successful military officer, famous for his defense of Gallipoli against the Allies during the First World War. In the chaos that followed the defeat of the Ottoman Empire in 1918, Kemal organised resistance to the last sultan, Mehmed VI, who was being used by the Allies to implement a peace that would have divided the Turkish-speaking lands of the former empire. In the Wars of Independence that followed, Atatürk established boundaries embracing most Turkish speakers – making culture rather than religion the basis for national identity, in a country that had for 300 years been ruled by sultans claiming to be caliphs, that is, civil and spiritual rulers of the Muslims.

Distancing his new country from the rival appeal of Islam was the guiding principle behind an extraordinary series of reforms enacted after he became president of the new Republic of Turkey in 1923. These included outlawing Arab dress (the fez was to be replaced by the panama) and the substitution of Latin for Arabic script, a move that further distanced future generations from their Islamic past.

Atatürk formulated six principles for the modern Turkish state, which were held to guide the revolution. They comprised his Republican People's Party election programme of 1931. Republicanism and populism came first, a simple defence of democracy against the return of traditional rulers. Then came

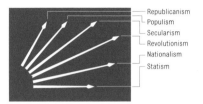

Right: Atatürk's six ruling principles are incorporated into the symbol of the Turkish Republican People's Party

- Republicanism
- Populism
- Secularism
- Revolutionism
- Nationalism
- Statism

nationalism and statism: Turkey was defined as a nation-state chiselled from the ruins of a multinational empire, independent from outside interference. It was united by a common language, shared values and culture, and open to every person born within the national boundaries regardless of race or religion. Finally, secularism and revolutionism overturned the religious and political power structures of the old order: Shari'a law was replaced with a legal code drawn from Italy, France and Germany. Women were emancipated and, by 1934, allowed to vote and stand for election. Divorce was legitimised. All citizens were equal in the eyes of the law.

The state became secular: all state influence on religion, and religious influence on the state (including education), was formally disavowed. Islam became one of many religions – a move formalised by the ending of the caliphate in March 1924. The state played an interventionist role, regulating economic activity and, in the drive for economic expansion, became the owner of the main enterprises. It also assumed some responsibility for social welfare.

Atatürk remains a revered figure in Turkey. State-revolution led by a one-party autocracy has been emulated, particularly in the Persia of the Shahs and in Egypt, but it has rarely had even the partial success Kemal Atatürk achieved in his own country.

Gamal Abdel Nasser

Gamal Abdel Nasser, president of Egypt from 1954 to 1970, envisioned a pan-Arab republic, free of colonial influence, that stretched from the Atlantic to the Red Sea. 'Nasserism' projected Egypt as both Arab and African, the bridge that linked the two, but was heavily reliant on the personality of Nasser himself and the brief glory that followed the Suez Crisis in 1956.

Born: 1918, Alexandria, Egypt
Importance: Promoted the concept of a pan-Arab republic
Died: 1970, Cairo, Egypt

The Second World War destabilised Egypt politically and socially. Pre-war attempts at secularising the state contributed to this instability. Both radical and right-wing movements were vying for power, including the Muslim Brotherhood, which was becoming an increasingly militant Islamic movement, while the creation of Israel in 1948 offered a cause around which the Arab world could unite.

Nasser, a soldier and hero of the first war against Israel in 1948, led the Free Officers, a military opposition movement that, in a 1952 anti-monarchist coup, put General Muhammad Naguib in power as the first president of the Egyptian Republic. In 1954, Nasser emerged from the shadows to become prime minister and effective ruler with the support of the trade unions and working classes, a power base that encouraged him to experiment with a form of Arab socialism.

In the same year, Nasser (backing Algerian rebels against the French) published *The Philosophy of the Revolution*, dismissed by the French Prime Minister, Guy Mollet, as 'Nasser's *Mein Kampf*'. In it, he portrayed a future in which the Arab nation would extend from Cairo to Damascus, Baghdad and Amman. It was a world awaiting a hero who would cleanse the region of foreign influence and build an ill-defined Islamic socialism, offering a third way between capitalism and Marxism.

The new Arab nation would lead the region's modernisation and build its ability to resist external intervention. It would also, Nasser hoped, direct some of the Arab world's oil resources in Egypt's direction. Like Atatürk a generation earlier (see pages 90–91), Nasser identified modernisation with industrialisation and economic growth.

He aspired to a secular, democratic and socialist future. Although he also aspired to lead the Islamic world, the move toward a pan-Arabism was intended to appeal to secular, pre-Islamic traditions rather than to religious unity.

'We can achieve much by Arab action, which is a main part of our battle. We must develop and build our countries to face the challenge of our enemies.'

Gamal Nasser, speech, 1967

Nasser introduced land reform and a ceiling on land holdings in an attempt to ease the poverty of rural Egypt and nationalised – 'Egyptized' – foreign companies, a move that had a catastrophic effect on inward investment. He secularised the religious schools. In response, in 1954, the Muslim Brotherhood sent an assassin who wounded Nasser (and provided him with an excuse to execute or imprison its leadership).

The 1956 Suez Crisis, and the humiliation of Britain and France, left Nasser the hero of the Arab world. On the crest of this wave, in 1958, he created the United Arab Republic, a first step to the pan-Arab nation, uniting Egypt with Syria. It lasted until 1961 when Syria seceded. But Nasser never abandoned his ambition and looked for causes around which he could unite other Arab states until his death in 1970.

Mahatma Gandhi

The father of modern India, Mohandas Karamchand Gandhi (known as Mahatma, or 'Great Soul') espoused principles of non-violence to achieve political and social reform. His methods have inspired anti-colonial and anti-racist movements ever since.

Born: 1869, Porbandar, India
Importance: Introduced concepts of passive resistance and non-violent protest to the political arena
Died: 1948, Delhi, India

As a young man, Gandhi went to London to study law where, in his efforts to keep his promise to his devout mother to eat no meat, he became a leading figure in the then intellectually fashionable vegetarian movement. He also read for the first time – in English – the Hindu poem the *Bhagavad Gita*, which later came to be his spiritual dictionary.

Three principles guided his life. *Satyagraha*, or 'truth force', literally the obstinate pursuit of truth, which he translated into non-violent resistance. This idea was reinforced by *aparigraha*, non-possessiveness, or selflessness. The third was *samabhava*, equanimity in the face of trial.

As a young lawyer in South Africa, Gandhi was at the forefront of the fight against laws that imposed humiliating restrictions on non-Europeans. In the course of his campaigns, he developed concepts of passive resistance and non-violent protest into powerful political weapons that exploited the colonial rulers' sense of their own moral purpose.

Gandhi always insisted he was no politician. His concern, he said, was the human spirit and the personal search for God. Influenced by the anti-capitalism of John Ruskin and the Christian fundamentalism of Leo Tolstoy, Gandhi came to dislike the materialism of modern capitalism as well as the indignities it imposed on the working classes and began developing other, simpler ways of life.

Back in India after 1914, he gave up Western dress and wore only Indian clothes made from homespun cotton. He became celibate, challenging himself by taking beautiful young women to lie beside him, and sought a model existence on the self-sufficient farm or *ashram* he established.

After the First World War he launched a campaign against proposals for imprisonment without trial, triggering a violent response culminating in the Amritsar massacre in which 400 Indians died. Still insisting he was motivated only by his personal search for truth, he transformed the Indian National Congress Party, preaching to the rural masses that their country's status was not the fault of the British but was due to imperfections in Indians themselves.

He instigated a boycott of all British institutions and defied British law. Thousands went to prison, including Gandhi. From 1930, Gandhi became committed to complete independence. He led a new *satyagraha* against the salt tax that led to the arrest of more than 60,000 before quitting politics again to campaign for rural education and against the notion of 'untouchability'.

In 1942 he returned to the national stage, demanding immediate British withdrawal from India. In the final years of empire, he tried to use fasts to end mounting communal violence but he could not prevent partition. Independence was finally granted on August 15, 1947. The following January 30, Gandhi was assassinated.

Passive resistance: Defiance of the political status quo by explicitly non-violent means, such as non-cooperation and peaceful protest. By simply refusing to comply with the dictates of government, a group of sufficient size can mount a serious challenge to the ruling power without resorting to violence, although such resistance is vulnerable to a violent response.

Nelson Mandela

After 27 years in prison, Nelson Mandela led South Africa through a peaceful revolution to democracy and became the Republic's first president. Promoting reconciliation with every act, he has become a symbol of the power of moral authority.

Born: 1918, Transkei, South Africa
Importance: South Africa's first president elected under black majority rule

Rolihlahia (later Nelson) Mandela came from rural South Africa to train as a lawyer in Johannesburg, where daily experience of the indignities of apartheid led him to join the African National Congress (ANC). Mandela's political philosophy was initially strongly influenced by Gandhi (see pages 94–95). Mandela first found himself on trial in 1956, after participating in the congress that approved the Freedom Charter, a declaration of intent to create a democratic, non-racist South Africa. The charter envisaged nationalised capitalist enterprises like banks and mines, and redistribution of the land.

The trial ended in 1961 with Mandela's acquittal. However, the ANC was banned and he was forced to operate in secret. After further repressive measures were introduced, the ANC decided to abandon peaceful protest. Mandela helped found the ANC's military wing, *Umkhonto we Sizwe*, the Spear of the Nation. Initially its intent was sabotage with the aim of undermining the South African economy. Anticipating escalating violence, Mandela underwent military training. He toured Africa and Europe looking for military and political support.

Mandela described himself as a socialist, partly because of his admiration for early African societies, where the land belonged to the tribe. He was also a convinced parliamentarian and supporter of the rule of law. The fight he waged in South Africa was against poverty and the lack of human dignity: socialism and majority rule were his solutions.

In 1964 he began a life term in the notoriously harsh Robben Island prison. Here he established a moral authority over his warders, threatening to take a violent warder to court and using his time there to turn the prison into the 'island university', denying the state the power to make him a victim.

From the mid-1980s, covert negotiations with the government began. But Mandela refused to accept anything other than virtual capitulation of the government. 'What freedom am I being offered while the organisation of the people remains banned?' In 1990, he was released from prison and the ANC was recognised once more.

Working tirelessly, the 72-year-old ex-prisoner persuaded his party to accept the need to cooperate with their old enemy. At moments of tension, for example when the ANC leader Chris Hani was assassinated, he restated his call for unity and reconciliation: 'Now is the time for all South Africans to stand together against those who from any quarter wish to destroy what Chris Hani gave his life for – the freedom of all of us.'

> 'I have fought against white domination, and I have fought against black domination. I have cherished the ideal of a democratic and free society in which all persons live together in harmony and with equal opportunities.'
>
> Nelson Mandela,
> at his trial in 1964

In 1994, in the country's first free elections, Mandela and the ANC were swept to power.

The Theocrat

Ayatollah Ruholla Khomeini

A Shia cleric, Khomeini overthrew Iran's Pahlavi dynasty in 1979, in a religious revolution to establish an anti-Western theocracy in Iran. His example has received praise and criticism in equal measure from Muslims across the world.

Born: 1900, Khomeyn, Iran
Importance: Staunchly anti-Western founder of the Islamic Republic of Iran
Died: 1989, Tehran, Iran

Khomeini (born Ruholla Musawi) first came to prominence protesting against Reza Shah Pahlavi's 1963 'White Revolution', a series of reforms that owed much to the ideas of Kemal Atatürk (see pages 90–91), secularising the law and the courts and introducing education and women's rights.

The clerics bitterly opposed reforms that not only diminished their power, but also the ability of ordinary Shiites to live what clerics considered godly lives. In 1963, Khomeini was exiled for criticising the Shah. Over the next fifteen years he developed the theory that shaped the revolution of 1979.

His most important ideas linked faith and politics into a doctrine called *velyat-e faqih*, 'the rule of the Islamic jurist', which he demanded replace the pro-Western government of the Shah. This was a break with Shiite teaching, which had called only for 'an openness' to clerical influence. As such it elevated the will of God, represented by the will of the clerics, above the will of the people, so legitimising what amounted to dictatorship.

The idea that the righteous must actively struggle against iniquitous government was heard in other Shiite communities in Iraq and Lebanon. Shiites, only about a fifth of the Muslim population, have often been an underclass. In Iran, thousands of rural poor were newly arrived in Tehran in search of work, separated from their families and villages, adrift in what was becoming a prosperous and sophisticated city.

Left: The basis of Khomeini's new republic was Islamic law — the Iranian Revolutionary coat of arms represents the name of Allah in Arabic script.

But there might have been no revolution had Khomeini not also won the attention of Iran's growing middle class, a group that had become frustrated by the Shah's reluctance to share power and his increasing reliance on repression and torture. Traditionally critical of the clerics, they saw in Khomeini's popularity the lever with which they might gain power.

Within weeks of the 1979 revolution, Khomeini declared an Islamic republic and took his breach with Shiite orthodoxy even further, requiring the state to enforce religious law. All secular opposition was excluded. Within a year, the new constitution, drawn up by clerics, proclaimed him political and religious leader for life and imposed a politically and socially conservative regime in which all authority derived from the leader, or *rahbar*.

Iran became a strictly observant society, requiring women to wear the veil, banning alcohol and Western music, and appointing clerics as policy makers. Khomeini abandoned Muhammad's respect for other faiths and preached Islamic unification and jihad.

Iran's 1979 constitution established the country as an Islamic republic and put into place a mixed system of government, in which a number of clergy-dominated bodies oversee the executive, parliament and judiciary, with the *rahbar* at the head of both the state and its overseeing institutions.

Wahhabism

Wahhabism is a puritan branch of Sunni Islam, dominant in the
kingdom of Saudi Arabia. In practice, it is the governing ideology
of what amounts to a theocracy – government based on religious
principles. Some of its adherents are linked with terrorism.

Wahhabism became the subject of intense controversy through its
involvement with fundamentalist Islamic movements in Chechnya
and the Balkans. Following 9/11, with 15 of the 19 hijackers of
Saudi origin, the entire sect was branded jihadist, unjustly many
Saudis would argue.

Wahhabism originated in the 18th century as an Islamic reform
movement that referred back to the early teachings of Muhammad.
Its founder, Muhammad ibn Abd al-Wahhab, believed Islam had
been corrupted partly by European influences, more by what he
regarded as the polytheistic practices of contemporary Islam that
would have been anathema to the prophet of the one true God.

Although recent scholarship has questioned it, Wahhabism is
particularly associated with an intolerant approach not only to non-
Muslims, but to non-Wahhabi Muslims. When Ibn Saud unified
Saudi Arabia in 1932, his army was composed of Wahhabi soldiers,
among whom there was a historic family alliance. It was Wahhabis
who conquered the diverse tribes of the desert land of Saudi Arabia
and delivered the territory to Ibn Saud. In return, Ibn Saud – now
King Abdul-Aziz – governed his kingdom according to a strictly
Islamic social order, with particular regard to education and justice.
In modern Saudi Arabia, both are conspicuously conservative.

Education is largely denied to women, while justice, based on
Sharia law, includes amputation. Contemporary questions such as
traffic violations are dealt with by royal decree. There is a rigorous
religious police force. The Koran is in effect the constitution,

although in 1992 a 'Basic Law' was proclaimed. The king combines in his person both legislative and executive powers. In so far as non-royal opinion is considered, it is partly through consultation with technical experts and partly through consultation with the *ulama*, or religious scholars.

The royal family's legitimacy is dependant on Wahhabism and Wahhabis are promoted to positions of authority by the royal family. In particular, the Saudi rulers rely on Wahhabis for internal security. But it is a more subtle relationship than such a broad-brush depiction allows. Wahhabism is not monolithic and the royal family exploits tensions within it.

As a theocracy and promoter of pan-Islamism, Saudi Arabia was hostile to the secular pan-Arabism promoted in the 1960s by Egypt's President Nasser. When Nasser moved against his domestic critics, the Muslim Brotherhood, they found refuge in the kingdom.

The Muslim Brotherhood originated from another Islamic reform movement, the Salafi. Although their concern was less a return to fundamentals than a desire to modernise, there was common ground with Wahhabism. The Egyptian exiles tended to be well educated – ideal candidates to answer oil-rich Saudi's growing need for teachers. Exposed to the secularism of some Arab powers, the Muslim Brotherhood had become increasingly hostile to Western influence, a hostility now entrenched in Saudi Arabia's education system. Saudi foreign policy has exported Wahhabi-Salafism since the anti-Soviet fight in Afghanistan in the decade after 1979.

The Taliban victory over the invaders, and the subsequent collapse of Soviet communism, was a powerful Islamic riposte to the humiliating failure of the secular Arab world against Israel in 1967 and (especially because of inept Western foreign policy) has embedded it in the politics of the region.

David Ben-Gurion

David Ben-Gurion, a leading Labor Zionist, played an important part in the creation of the state of Israel and was its first prime minister. *Time* magazine named him as one of the 100 most important people of the 20th century.

Born: 1886, Plonsk, Poland
Importance: Pivotal in the creation of Israel as a socialist Jewish state
Died: 1973, Tel Aviv, Israel

Ben-Gurion was born David Gruen in eastern Poland, then part of the Russian Empire, at a time of rising anti-Semitism. It was also the age of European cultural and political nationalism, of empire and colonialism, and the slow rise of the working class. Ben-Gurion made a significant contribution to the fusion of all these ideas into a political philosophy that directed and defined Jewish objectives in Palestine.

The idea of a homeland where Europe's Jews could escape persecution and reclaim their historic territory was well established by the time Ben-Gurion, aged 20, first went to Palestine to farm on the shores of the Sea of Galilee. The following year, the Poale Zion – the party of political Zionism – adopted the objective of political independence for Jews in Palestine. The Balfour Declaration of 1917 appeared to commit the Allied powers to supporting the quest for a Jewish homeland.

Ben-Gurion was the first secretary of Histadrut, a Jewish workers' organisation that became the driving force behind his vision and of his own Mifleget Poalei Eretz Israel, or Land of Israel Worker's Party, forerunner of the Israeli Labor Party. Ben-Gurion saw Histadrut as a way to organise Jewish immigrants, arriving in great numbers from Europe throughout the 1920s and 1930s, into the nucleus of a socialist Jewish state.

Determined to respect the traditions of European liberalism, he envisaged Jewish and Arab workers uniting to promote their shared economic objectives, while remaining culturally distinct in order to further their political ambitions. Later, he was accused of proposing a kind of apartheid, but he demanded that Arabs be

'In Israel, in order to be a realist you must believe in miracles.'

David Ben-Gurion,
interview 1956

treated as equals, with open cultural exchange as befitted allies in the class struggle. Yet his hope of deflecting Arab nationalism from conflict with Zionism through the offer of material prosperity was defeated when the influx of Jews was more than matched by an influx of Arabs as British military and commercial activity brought a first taste of prosperity to Palestine.

Histadrut, under Ben-Gurion's control, became the second most powerful institution in the British Mandate of Palestine, operating as a state within a state, an essential tool intended to unite the waves of immigrants around the objective of a Jewish nation of free and equal individuals. However, Britain's pro-Arabism during the Second World War led Ben-Gurion in the 1940s to develop his idea of 'fighting Zionism'.

Fighting Zionism offered a way to suppress cultural differences and unite the thousands of Jews who fled Europe during and after the war. In its name, Ben-Gurion ruthlessly overcame the internal divisions of the private militias of rival leaders that threatened civil war. At the same time, his elevation of Israel's historic claim to Palestine, ended by the Romans 2,000 years earlier, provided another rallying point for many religious Jews. But in power as prime minister from the founding of the state in 1948 to 1953 and again from 1955 to 1963, he was more pragmatist than philosopher, relying on Western support against Arab hostility.

Mao Tse-tung

Chairman Mao ruthlessly shaped modern China, using a cult of personality, cruelty and terror that caused millions to die through famine and persecution. He led the Chinese Communist Party from 1931, and the Chinese People's Republic from 1949 until 1959. He remained its major influence until his death.

Born: 1893, Hunan Province, China
Importance: Founder of the Chinese People's Republic – a communist regime
Died: 1976, Beijing, China

From farming stock, Mao grew up during the turmoil caused by the collapse of the last imperial dynasty. He fought in Sun Yat-sen's first revolt in 1911 (see pages 84–85) and was a founding member of the Chinese Communist Party in 1921. In the war with Chiang Kai-shek from 1928, he led a Red Army faction and retreated with them on the Long March to northern China in 1934. He emerged as leader only in the 1940s. His experience as a soldier and his combative outlook led him to lean heavily on military support for the rest of his life.

Lacking the experience of some of his contemporaries and the intellectual gifts of others, Mao proclaimed that his policies rested on his knowledge of China itself. He saw early that the peasants, rather than industrial workers, might be the source of his power, and the success of his military tactics, encircling cities from the countryside, depended on their support. Ever the pragmatist, when Japan invaded in the 1930s, Mao was conciliatory to his old enemy, the Kuomintang, while in the 1940s, he restored communist leadership in an anti-imperialist proletarian revolution.

Starting in the late 1930s, Mao developed ideas about the 'sinification' of Marxism, a rejection of aspects of Soviet Marxism that he felt failed to meet Chinese conditions. He envisaged a union between intellectual and physical effort through which China

Above: In a country like China with a relatively low level of industrialisation, revolution must come from the agrarian rather than the industrial proletariat.

could defeat poverty and reach the sunlit uplands of socialism. After 1949, Mao led China back to orthodoxy, subordinating rural interests to a campaign of industrialisation – only to reject the rigid bureaucracy that was required to police it. In the late 1950s he launched the Great Leap Forward, an accelerated five-year plan intended to replace industrial advance by using manpower alone to boost productivity, while encouraging every town and village to develop small-scale industry.

Doctrinally pure brigades replaced experts in charge of local decision-making in what Mao hoped would see a revival of the egalitarian simplicity of his years as a soldier. Instead, perhaps 20 million people died of hunger, to add to the 20 million killed during the revolution. In 1961, the policy was reversed.

The Cultural Revolution that began in the mid-1960s emerged from Mao's belief that 'capitalist roaders' were taking the economy in the wrong direction. It also served to restructure the party, helpfully disposing of political rivals and critics. Anti-intellectualism was encouraged as an aspect of class war, which extolled peasant ignorance. Gradually, though, the experiment was revoked in favour of despotic centralism that lasted until Mao's death in 1976.

Muhammad

Within his lifetime, Muhammad established a religion able to capture an empire and unite the Arab nation, comprising unalterable laws governing man's relationship with God and society. Within a hundred years, the Islamic religion was established across Arabia and North Africa, and had spread into southern Europe and Asia.

Born: 570, Mecca, Arabia
Importance: Founder of Islam
Died: 632, Medina, Arabia

Muhammad was an orphan of a branch of the Quraysh, the ruling tribe of Mecca. From his youth, he began to have visions. Charismatic, esteemed for his sense of justice and his devout way of life, only when he reached 40 did the process of Koranic revelation – which continued for the rest of his life – begin.

The central message was the oneness of God and rejection of idolatory, teachings that set Muhammad and his growing band of followers in opposition to the authorities of Mecca, guardians of the holy shrine of Kaaba. In 622, in the *hegira* or 'migration', Muhammad fled to what would become Medina.

There he became the channel for continued Koranic revelation and the ruler of an expanding community of disparate tribes to whom he gave a system of laws and government derived from God. Although much developed after Muhammad's death, the principles of Islam were laid down in his lifetime.

In the face of early persecution, faith and community were intimately linked: revelation dictated both an individual's relationship with God and with society. In Medina, Muhammad drew up a constitution still regarded among Muslims as the ideal. The interests of the community were paramount. Its purpose was to promote good and destroy the evils of mischief and corruption. Social justice was its guiding principle and distinctions of birth and wealth were replaced by an equality in the eyes of God. Although slavery was not expressly banned, slaves were emancipated, women and children protected and girl infanticide outlawed. Only piety and good acts earned distinction. Although only 80 verses of the Koran actually deal with legal matters, other laws, governing diet, banning alcohol and regularising social institutions like marriage, were also introduced.

Without military success to ward off rival tribes, inspire loyalty and provide income from plunder, Muhammad's community could not have survived. At the same time, religious activism – jihad – was a central obligation of all followers. While maintaining a modest lifestyle, Muhammad became a tribal leader, engaged in diplomacy (often reinforced through marriage) and sometimes conflict, rewarding his followers with the spoils of raids – and levying a tax, the *zakat*, to meet the needs of the poor.

Jerusalem, the initial focus of worship, was hostile. Instead, Mecca became the centre of Islam and the new Arab world that was to be created. By 630, after years of opposition, Mecca fell without a struggle and joined the new religion. Part of the initial success of Islam lay in its rejection of traditional tribal loyalty. To join the community, it was only necessary to follow Muhammad's teachings. He also allowed a degree of religious pluralism, taxing people of other faiths but recognising Christians and Jews as 'people of the book' and banning conversion by force.

'Even as the fingers of the two hands are equal, so are human beings equal to one another. No one has any right, nor any preference to claim over another. You are brothers.'

Final sermon of Muhammad

Abraham Lincoln

Abraham Lincoln was the 16th president of the United States and is widely regarded as its greatest. He ended slavery, held the Union together with victory in the Civil War and helped found the Republican Party. His speeches remain the subject of debate by successors anxious to claim his authority.

Born: 1809, Hodgenville, Kentucky
Importance: America's greatest president, bringing an end to slavery and promoting government of the people, by the people, for the people
Died: 1865, Washington D.C.

The son of poor farmers, Lincoln's political ambition led him, still in his 20s, to become an Illinois state legislator for the Whigs, and soon afterward to qualify as a lawyer. In 1846 he became a congressman.

Slavery in 19th-century America raised many questions to tax political theorists: the origin of law, the rights of minorities, the resolution of differences in a democracy and the moral purpose of the state. Lincoln held that the constitution's principles pre-dated the constitution itself: the principle that all were born equal, and had the right to be ruled only with their consent, made slavery wrong. But because the constitution did not expressly prohibit slavery, individual states had to be allowed to continue it. Lincoln treated the constitution with lawyerly respect and a shrewd political calculation that led him to seek the widest possible consensus before introducing the amendment to emancipate the slaves.

Lincoln thought slavery not only an injustice but also an economic handicap. Free labour and free soil – the right for settlers to make their own futures – were his guiding principles. Faced with a choice between democratic doctrinal purity and moral and economic advance, he opposed the 1854 Kansas-Nebraska Act that would allow slavery in the new territories of the United States wherever the principle of popular sovereignty sanctioned it.

Despite losing the argument, he won the Republican presidential nomination and in November 1860 became its first president-elect. Before he took office, a number of southern states seceded from the Union to form the Confederacy. Within weeks of his inauguration, the Civil War had begun.

The war, lasting from 1861 to 1865, saw Lincoln's greatest distillation of American constitutionalism. He sought to leave open the way to peace throughout and declared that he was neither for nor against slavery where it existed, only with preserving the Union. In the 1863 Emancipation Proclamation, he declared slaves free but only in Confederate-held states.

Only 200,000 of about four million slaves were thus freed but as a symbol it was invaluable. It turned the war into a crusade, uniting the Union's forces and attracting international support. It also marked the centralisation of presidential power, as Lincoln added to the powers he had taken as commander in chief to garner enough support to turn the proclamation into the 13th amendment.

In his most celebrated speech, the Gettysburg Address in the autumn of 1863, Lincoln took just 271 words to express the war aims of the Union: the preservation of a free nation and 'government of the people, by the people, for the people'.

Having won both the civil war and another term, his second inaugural address promised a peace with 'malice towards none; with charity towards all'. Weeks later he was assassinated.

Civil rights: Protected freedoms guaranteed to the individual by the laws of his nation, as opposed to human rights which are held to be universal, independent of political power. Civil rights movements have historically been dedicated to ensuring that all citizens have equal rights under the law.

Charles de Gaulle

Charles de Gaulle rallied resistance to the Nazi occupation of France after May 1940 and led the 'free French' into Paris in 1944. He became France's first peacetime president but resigned in protest at the weakness of the constitution in 1946. In 1958, he became the first president of the Fifth Republic.

Born: 1890, Lille, France
Importance: Pursued a nationalist and anti-imperialist course in restoring 'grandeur' to post-war France
Died: 1970, Colombey les Deux Eglises, France

Son of a Jesuit schoolmaster, de Gaulle fought with distinction in the First World War before being taken prisoner. Returning to military duty, he won a reputation for unorthodoxy and thoughtfulness, speaking and writing about the nature of leadership as well as the need to modernise and professionalise the army.

As German forces closed in on Paris and Marshal Petain prepared for an armistice, de Gaulle fled to London. From there he broadcast to occupied France with the romantic pragmatism that distinguished his political appeal, proclaiming that 'honour, common sense, and the interest of the nation' demanded resistance.

First from London and then from Algeria, de Gaulle built a coalition inside and outside France, ensuring that France itself had a major role in regaining her freedom. Similarly, his insistence that General Eisenhower liberate Paris early in the campaign pre-empted plans to impose an allied military government.

But de Gaulle, convinced of the need for a constitution that supported strong leadership, fell out with the politicians and in 1946 he quit politics. It took 12 years of colonial uprising and economic and social uncertainty before crisis led to his recall.

In his wilderness years, de Gaulle developed the political outlook that became Gaullism. At its heart was a France free from foreign influence, politically and culturally. Domestically, he sought a third way between socialism and capitalism.

By 1958, de Gaulle was able to set his own terms for a return to power. He insisted on enhancing the powers of the president, and in 1962 he controversially amended his Fifth Constitution to introduce direct elections for the presidency.

'Yes, it is Europe, from the Atlantic to the Urals, it is Europe, it is the whole of Europe, that will decide the fate of the world.'

Charles de Gaulle, speech 1959

Acting in a semi-monarchical style, he set out to restore 'grandeur'. He distanced France from the growing global network of military and economic alliances. Although he fulfilled the commitment to the European Economic Community (EEC), he opposed any attempt to impinge on national powers (except in respect of the Common Agricultural Policy that greatly benefitted French farmers). He resisted British entry on the grounds that it would introduce American influence, and withdrew from NATO's military command. In order to pursue an explicitly French foreign policy, he sought an independent nuclear weapon.

More immediately, he dealt with the pressing problem of Algerian independence, recognising that ambitions for a French Algeria were unsustainable. Granting self-determination to France's African colonies, and travelling to Canada to cry 'Vive le Quebec libre', he became a champion of anti-imperialism.

In 1968, student and worker protests broke out across the country. As the crisis peaked, de Gaulle declared he had military support to suppress any anarchistic or communist uprising. Calm was restored, concessions made. The following year, his proposals for further constitutional reform were rejected and he resigned.

The War Lord

Sir Winston Churchill

As prime minister of Britain from 1940 to 1945, Sir Winston Churchill led the defence of democracy and the free world against fascism. Prime minister again from 1961 to 1965, it is as a war leader that he remains most celebrated.

Born: 1874, Blenheim, England

Importance: Championed democracy over tyranny, motivating many in the fight against Hitler's fascism.

Died: 1965, London, England

Born into nobility, Churchill's undistinguished school days gave way to a glittering career, first as a flamboyant soldier, then as a politician and, before he was 35, cabinet minister.

As a politician, Churchill actively sought enemies just as a soldier needed a foe. His enemy of choice was communism, a term that for him covered many moderate socialists and trade unionists too. As pressure for Indian home rule mounted, even Gandhi (see pages 94–95) joined the list of the unacceptable.

Churchill was a great Tory democrat. In peacetime, democracy was a freedom that had to be earned and that could be exercised only in specific conditions. The empire was a protector of the rights of all its subjects in preparation for a distant future when all men would be capable of self-rule. How and when that happened was not of interest to Churchill.

Despite moves from the Conservatives to the Liberals and back again, Churchill would claim that his principles never changed. 'Socialism seeks to pull down wealth. Liberalism seeks to raise up poverty. . . . Socialism exalts the rule; Liberalism exalts the man. Socialism attacks capital, Liberalism attacks monopoly.'

Churchill, out of office in the 1930s, saw the danger of Hitler's remilitarisation of Germany from a historical perspective: a single dominant European power had always been against British interests. The terror of modern warfare never fazed

Left: Churchill saw the British Empire as protector of its subject nations, nurturing their development until they became capable of just and peaceful self-rule.

Churchill and his own 'finest hour' (the phrase he coined in 1940 to describe the Battle of Britain) came as war leader. His extraordinary rhetoric, global in reach, defined the nature of the challenge posed by Hitler and the Nazis and the free world's response to it.

To rally support for a war that not everyone saw as in his self-interest, he offered a vision of democracy as an ideal in opposition to tyranny. Democratic countries, he suggested, were brothers-in-arms so close that they could be fellow citizens (an idea he actually proposed, first to France and then to the United States). It was his repeated public urging to America to come to democracy's aid that ultimately transcended traditional hostility to Britain as an imperial power and around which he built a coalition that included even campaigners for Indian independence.

The idea of the war as a struggle for freedom was persuasive enough to survive even the alliance with Stalin, a tyrant to match Hitler. Churchill called it an alliance between peoples and that image was sustained by costly shipments of provisions to the beleaguered and sometimes besieged Soviet people.

With the war over, Churchill, intent on sustaining America as defender of European democracy, warned of the iron curtain the Soviets had drawn across Europe. For the rest of his career, his concern was to protect democracy by containing communism.

Democracy

Literally the 'rule of the people', democracy is widely considered the best (or possibly merely the least bad) form of government for the modern world. It protects individual freedoms and allows all citizens to exercise both the right and the moral responsibility to participate in government.

Theories of democracy begin in 400 BC with Pericles, whose funeral oration contains the earliest description of a democratic state: 'Its administration favours the many instead of the few; this is why it is called a democracy. If we look to the laws, they afford equal justice to all in their private differences.' It was a system blind to wealth or class, sustained by written and inalienable rights.

Democracy poses several challenges: Who is entitled to vote? What happens where majority rule does not prevail? How are minorities protected? It requires a settled constitution, a peaceful environment and an electorate prepared to tolerate defeat.

Contemporary democracy is unrecognisable from the Aristotelian concept of a democracy limited to full citizens (perhaps a tenth of the population) within the boundaries of a city-state. But it was Aristotle who expressly made the link between democracy and individual liberty that was taken up by Locke in the 17th century. His work in turn influenced the American constitution, while in France Baron de Montesquieu noted the importance of a body motivated by the concept of public good.

In the 19th century the libertarian John Stuart Mill offered a definition of the basic freedoms that government must protect. A century later, John Rawls questioned liberal democracy's principle of the 'greatest good for the greatest number' and argued instead that equality, or social justice, should be its first concern. Abraham Lincoln's famous proposition that government should be 'of the people, by the people, for the people' implies a far more complex system of support than its simplicity suggests.

One practical turning point was England's civil war, and the acceptance that involvement in government might be delegated to representatives between elections. England's evolution by the late 18th century from monarchy to a limited democracy provided the practical solution to many theoretical problems.

The theoretical breakthrough was the acceptance of liberty and equality. Before the British system was democratised, the United States constructed its own democratic system of government inspired by French revolutionary ideas and based on the inalienable rights of the individual.

Democracy's great strength is its capacity to accommodate different political systems: as long as sovereignty remains with the people, the complexion of the government might range across the spectrum from libertarian to socialist. But every government is tempered by the source of its legitimacy – the people themselves.

Democratic support can be measured using various systems. Where the geographic principle outweighs precise party support, 'winner takes all' is the best method. For each vote cast to have the greatest influence, some form of proportional representation is fairer. Often variations on the two systems are used to elect different tiers of government within one country.

In this era of global terror, the liberties on which democracy rests are under attack in the name of security. The priority of personal security over personal freedom does battle with the fears of the people. At the same time, the inequalities magnified by wide-scale immigration and the triumph of liberal economics challenge another precondition of successful democracy, equal access to resources.

Martin Luther King Jr.

As leader of the civil rights movement in the United States from the 1950s, Martin Luther King Jr. successfully campaigned against legal segregation and inspired generations of black and white Americans to fight the injustices with which they lived.

Born: 1929, Atlanta, Georgia
Importance: Championed non-violent protest in his campaign for equal rights for black and white
Died: 1968, Memphis, Tennessee

King was the son of an Atlanta pastor, raised in comfort. But it was impossible to remain ignorant of the inequality between black and white and he grew up in the social gospel tradition: the teaching of Christ compelled action wherever injustice prevailed.

Trained as a pastor himself, King's first campaign was against segregation on public transport in Montgomery, Alabama. After Rosa Parks was arrested for refusing to give up her seat to a white passenger, he led a public transport boycott with a speech that heralded a new era of protest: 'For many years we have shown an amazing patience. . . . But we come here tonight to be saved from that patience that makes us patient with anything less than freedom and justice.'

His success in Montgomery helped him build the Southern Christian Leadership Conference as the base for what became first a national and then an international campaign for justice between black and white. He was influenced by both the struggle for colonial freedom in Africa and India's struggle for independence. A visit to Nehru in India (see pages 124–125) stimulated his interest in Gandhian non-violent resistance. Civil disobedience, the act of breaking a law and accepting the punishment in order to make a protest, became a key weapon in his campaigns.

King had a powerful sense of his own motivation. 'I refuse to accept despair as the final response to the ambiguities of history. I refuse to accept the idea that the "isness" of man's present nature makes him morally incapable of reaching up for the eternal "oughtness" that forever confronts him.'

The new medium of television and the rising aspirations of an increasingly prosperous nation provided King with the ideal platform. In 1963, in front of 200,000 gathered at the Lincoln Memorial in the name of equal justice for all, King electrified the crowd with his most famous speech: 'I have a dream.'

In 1964 the Civil Rights Act allowed federal government to enforce non-segregation. That autumn, King won the Nobel Peace Prize. 'Non-violence,' he said, 'is the answer to the crucial political and moral question of our time – the need for man to overcome oppression and violence without resorting to violence and oppression.' In 1965, the Voting Rights Act gave legal support to the enfranchisement of blacks in the south.

In the final years of his life, King came under attack from more radical black leaders like Malcolm X for what they felt was the timidity of non-violent resistance. He was accused of communist subversion by some in the Washington establishment, especially after he joined the campaign against the Vietnam War and extended his campaigning to include poverty.

King was assassinated in Memphis in 1968. 'I may not get there with you,' he said the night before he died, 'but I want you to know tonight that we, as a people, will get to the promised land.'

> 'One has not only a legal, but a moral responsibility to obey just laws. Conversely, one has a moral responsibility to disobey unjust laws.'
>
> Dr. Martin Luther King Jr., letter 1963

Lech Walesa

Lech Walesa was a shipyard worker who liberated Poland from communism through Solidarity, the first independent trade union in a country that was part of the communist bloc. His leadership contributed to the collapse of the Soviet Empire itself.

Born: 1943, Wloclawek, Poland
Importance: Liberated Poland from the autonomy of communist Russia.

Lech Walesa was trained as an electrician at the Lenin Shipyard in Gdansk on the Baltic. As a boy, he witnessed the 1956 food riots; as a young man, he witnessed their repeat in 1970, when police shot dead dozens of demonstrators. In 1976, he lost his job for his involvement in further anti-government riots.

In August 1980, the government tried once more to raise food prices. The Gdansk workers went on strike and Walesa joined them (by breaking into the blockaded shipyard) and became their chief negotiator. The strike spread and, by October, Solidarity had been formed, an alliance of trade unions, intellectuals and anti-government forces throughout Poland.

Walesa, young and fit with a walrus moustache that made him instantly identifiable around the world, relished his audience and they loved his flamboyance and unadorned integrity. He was a deeply religious Catholic whose spirits, like those of millions of his countrymen, had been raised when, in 1978, their Cardinal Karol Wojtyla became Pope John Paul II. In 1979, the Pope paid a historic visit to his native land. Walesa has always credited the Pope with begining the chain of events that led to the downfall of communism.

The Pope reminded Poles of what it meant to be Polish and provided a bridge between workers and intellectuals that made Solidarity possible. The union was far more than just a workers' organisation, although its origins in the shipyards lent it credibility.

Solidarity's membership covered the spectrum from Christian Democrat to Polish Communist.

Walesa brought Poles together through his ability to respond to their unspoken emotions, and his courage in the face of a government that was prepared to use any means against its opponents. He was ordinary enough to appeal to every worker, extraordinary enough to hold together the disparate anti-communist elements in Solidarity.

'They could kill us but they could not defeat us. They could disperse us but they could not force us to work. So in fact the Communists did not have very effective weapons to use.'

Lech Walesa, interview with Mike Donkin, 2005

In the middle of 1981, Solidarity appeared unstoppable. By the end of 1981 it appeared crushed, its leaders including Walesa in jail, telephones disconnected, martial law imposed. But in truth, Solidarity was unstoppable. In the shadow of its memory, the government could never restore its legitimacy. In 1984 Walesa accepted the Nobel Peace Prize – in absentia, for he could not travel. In June 1989, Solidarity swept to power in the first elections and, in 1990, Lech Walesa became president in the first direct elections.

The qualities that had made him so effective a leader of a peaceful insurgency were less well fitted to the presidency. His social conservatism was against the spirit of the times and the confrontational style that had cowed the communist authorities seemed like bullying in a democracy. Standing for a second term in 1995, he was defeated.

Fidel Castro

Castro, Cuba's Marxist dictator since 1959, led the first communist regime in the Western hemisphere. He sought to spread revolution across Latin America and Africa and in old age is the hero of other Latin American radicals such as Venezuela's Hugo Chavez.

Born: 1926, Biran, Cuba
Importance: Pioneer of communism in the West

Born the illegitimate son of a relatively prosperous family, Fidel Castro was attracted to revolutionary politics from his university days. He was involved in a plot to overthrow the dictator of the Dominican Republic, and then an uprising in Colombia before, in 1953, leading a vain attack on the barracks in Santiago de Cuba in response to the seizure of power by General Batista. He spent the next two years in prison.

Exiled in Mexico, he set up the 26th of July Movement in honour of the attack and trained a guerrilla force. In December 1956, accompanied by his brother Raul, Che Guevara and a small band of fighters, he landed in Cuba to combat the Batista regime. On January 1, 1959, after two years of intermittent warfare and highly effective propaganda, Batista was forced to flee.

Fleetingly it seemed the new government, formed from what had been a 'Junta of Unity' with support across Cuban society, might be populist and democratic. But Castro took power within six months, intent on introducing his own brand of Cuban Marxism. 'There is not Communism or Marxism, but representative democracy and social justice in a well-planned economy,' he said at the time. To the nearby United States, land nationalisation, the expropriation of American property, and one-party rule all looked remarkably like communism, and Soviet communism at that.

But Castro would claim intellectual descent from Simón Bolívar and the 19th-century Latin American liberationists (see pages 80–81), rejecting injustice wherever it occured, rather than trying to introduce a doctrinaire economic system.

Free health, education and welfare were introduced. Jobs for all were guaranteed. Cuba remains healthier and better educated than almost all other comparable developing countries. However, political dissent and opposition were suppressed. The prisons filled with Castro's critics. Thousands fled.

As US aid and markets faltered in the Cold War era, Castro turned to the Soviet Union. In response, the US sought to depose Castro and a disastrous attack by Cuban exiles at the Bay of Pigs was beaten off by Castro's forces; the Soviets meanwhile began to install ballistic missiles on Cuban soil. However, after the 1962 Cuban Missile Crisis caused near catastrophe, there was a kind of rapprochement between the superpowers.

Although Castro had deposed a corrupt regime that reduced millions of Cubans to poverty, his economic reforms – particularly without an American market for the island's principle export, sugarcane – failed to produce the returns he had both anticipated and needed to fund his ambitious welfare programme. The Soviets stepped in with a guarantee to buy the sugar crop at an inflated price.

In the 1980s, without ever succeeding in making Cuba non-aligned, Castro became a leader of the non-aligned world. But the collapse of Soviet communism led to a withdrawal of aid and he was forced to accept a degree of free-market activity. In the twilight of his regime, he has won new popularity in Latin America, the region he longed to revolutionise.

Planned economy:
Economic system associated with socialism whereby the government controls the flow of capital, often nationalising industry, supporting unprofitable enterprises to maintain employment levels, and controlling production and supply of goods by quota.

Mikhail Gorbachev

In just six years, Mikhail Gorbachev ended the Cold War and embarked on a courageous series of economic and political reforms. He allowed Eastern Europe to escape the Soviet bloc because he wanted the USSR to 'stop throwing its weight about' but failed in his aim of holding together the Soviet Union.

Born: 1931, Stavropol, USSR
Importance: Brought an end to the Cold War

Gorbachev was the son of peasant farmers in the Stavropol region in the southwest of what is now the Russian Federation. His political talents were spotted while working as a farmhand and, in 1952, he went to Moscow's law school. By 1970 he was first secretary of the regional Communist party and in 1980 was a full member of the Politburo at a youthful 49 years old.

Gorbachev had been a student in Moscow when Stalin died, and later witnessed Krushchev's attempts to reform not just the international scene with his proposal for peaceful coexistence with the West, but also the domestic economy.

Gorbachev became the party's General Secretary in 1985. Through his travels, he knew how far behind the standards of the West the people of the USSR were. He also understood that the economy was crippled by the demands of the military that took a quarter of the country's gross national profit.

On accepting the Nobel Peace Prize in 1990, he quoted Kant who prophesied that mankind would one day be faced with a dilemma: 'either to be joined in a true union of nations or to perish in a war of annihilation ending in the extinction of the human race.' He felt that the world was at the moment of truth.

Originally he hoped 'New Thinking' – including removing nuclear weapons from Europe – might save the existing system. He understood that Russia's economic future lay in innovation

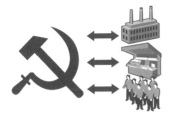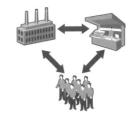

Above: The Soviet government controlled the flow of capital in its planned economy. *Perestroika* left the economy open to private enterprise and market forces.

and free thought. But the *perestroika* and *glasnost* – economic restructuring and transparency in government – that he led were unable to prevent the collapse of the Soviet economy. Indeed, Gorbachev himself seemed to have no clear idea of how to deconstruct a centrally planned economy. 'We want to be an integral part of modern civilization,' he said. 'To live in harmony with mankind's universal values, abide by the norms of international law, follow the "rules of the game" in our economic relations with the outside world.'

The New Thinking was less a sudden liberalisation than an attempt to provide an alternative orthodoxy. Despite his Western-style charm and youthful energy, Gorbachev insisted that he remained a Marxist-Leninist. His hope was to achieve reform so that the Soviet economy could again challenge that of the West, and the USSR be a real superpower again.

But he fought a tradition that resolved differences with repression or bloodshed. He had too little time to put his reforms into practice. The economic dislocation it caused stirred hostility and he was torn between conservatives and radicals like his ultimate successor, Boris Yeltsin. On December 25, 1991, Gorbachev dissolved the Soviet Union. 'The Cold War has ended,' he said. 'We live in a new world.'

Great Leaders

Jawaharlal Nehru

One of the leaders of the Indian independence movement, Nehru became India's first prime minister in 1947 and a noted exponent of the idea of non-alignment in foreign affairs. His daughter, Indira, and later his grandson, Rajiv, also became prime ministers.

Born: 1889, Allahabad, India
Importance: India's first prime minister
Died: 1964, New Delhi, India

Jawaharlal Nehru once joked that he was the last Englishman to rule India: the son of a well-to-do family of traditional lawyers and administrators, he was educated at Harrow and Cambridge in the UK and trained as a barrister.

Soon after he returned to India, he and his father became part of Gandhi's circle, attracted by his demand to resist the wrongs of Indian subjugation (see pages 94–95). In the cause, Nehru travelled widely to see the poverty of rural India. A visit to Europe and the USSR in the mid-1920s convinced him that the answer lay in gradualist Fabian socialism and economic planning.

Gandhi exploited the young Nehru's radicalism to attract other younger and more intellectual supporters. Nehru rose rapidly to positions of power within the Congress Party, becoming its chairman in 1929. From the mid-1930s, he was Gandhi's acknowledged successor.

On nine occasions Nehru was imprisoned by the British. Even so, he remained an Anglophile, although he reluctantly supported Gandhi's call for the immediate withdrawal of Britain in 1942, prompting a final period of detention for the entire Congress leadership. As a result, the alternative party, Jinnah's Muslim League, was left inadequately challenged. Partition, which secularist Nehru and Gandhi opposed, became harder to prevent.

From 1947, as the first prime minister of the world's largest democracy, Nehru declared politics and religion obsolete in favour of science and spirituality. Paternalist more than idealist, he introduced 'state-led' socialism: along with democracy, unity and secularism, it was the guiding principle, intended to deliver the modernisation needed to bring prosperity to the people.

'A moment comes, which comes but rarely in history, when we step out from the old to the new, when an age ends, and when the soul of a nation, long suppressed, finds utterance.'

Prime Minister Jawaharlal Nehru, inaugural address, 1947

Instead it illustrated the weakness of an imposed transformation. Social reform policies made no difference to attitudes to women or untouchables. State-run industry was bureaucratic and inefficient. He also relied heavily – too heavily, his critics say – on institutions inherited from the British, in particular the police and the military, and on senior British advisers. Foreign aid became more and more vital to sustaining the economy. However, he did found the Institutes of Technology, which have become nurseries for India's technical revolution.

He was more comfortable, although little more successful, trying to chart a course between East and West in foreign affairs, developing the concept of non-alignment that the West interpreted as pro-Soviet. But when China unexpectedly invaded, the West answered the appeal for help and forced a Chinese retreat.

Whatever the criticisms now made of Nehru's 17 years in power, with his integrity and social concern and his ability to speak the same political language as the imperialist British, he successfully oversaw the introduction of what has proved an enduring independent democracy.

Barack Obama

On November 4, 2008, Barack Obama ushered in a new era in American politics when he defeated John McCain, his Republican opponent, to become the first black president of the United States. Obama's ascent to the highest office has been meteoric. Four years ago, he was a relative unknown when he thrilled the Democratic National Convention with a speech that stressed the importance of high aspirations and self-reliance, and in which he noted that his father had originally come to America because it was known to be a beacon of freedom and opportunity for all.

Born: 1961, Honolulu, Hawaii
Importance: First African-American president of the USA less than 50 years after the civil rights movement.

Obama is the child of a Kenyan man and a white woman from Kansas. He was raised by his grandparents in Hawaii, and went on to study political science at Columbia University, and then law at Harvard Law School, where he became the first black president of the Harvard Law Review. He worked as a community organizer and civil rights lawyer in Chicago, and became an Illinois state senator in 1996.

His politics are broadly liberal. He was an early critic of the Iraq War, and during the 2008 presidential campaign made much of his plans to offer health care for all and to reduce carbon emissions. However, he also espouses a strong belief in a post-partisan politics, suggesting that it is necessary to reach out to voters of all political persuasions. It is notable then that his presidential candidacy was backed by Republican luminaries such as Colin Powell and Scott McClellan (a former spokesman for George Bush).

Obama's political career, although remarkably successful to date, has not been entirely free of controversy. In particular, he attracted criticism for his links with the Trinity United Church of Christ in Chicago, after it emerged that its former pastor, the

Rev. Jeremiah Wright, had said of the terrorist atrocities of 9/11 that they were like 'chickens coming home to roost', and also that America had a history of treating black people as 'less than human', for which it should be damned.

In response to the criticism that came his way, Obama insisted that it was no good pretending that the issue of race didn't exist and that the anger felt by many black people was manufactured. To do so, he argued, would serve only to widen the chasm of misunderstanding that exists between the races.

Obama's victory in the 2008 presidential election sparked celebrations around the world. It was remarkable not only in that it represented the culmination of a process of black empowerment that had begun with the civil rights movement some 50 years previously, but also in that his candidacy and election campaign had enthused people, especially the young, in a way unmatched in recent American political history. His use of Internet marketing strategies to promote awareness and galvanize support played a significant role in his success and will provide a model for future campaigns.

In Chicago, 120,000 people gathered in Grant Park to hear him declare that his victory would be a defining moment of real change for America. Some two months later, this was the theme that dominated his inauguration speech:

> Starting today, we must pick ourselves up, dust ourselves off, and begin again the work of remaking America. We will build the roads and bridges, the electric grids and digital lines that feed our commerce and bind us together . . . All this we can do. All this we will do.

History, of course, will judge whether Obama's presidency is a success. For now, it is enough to celebrate him as the first black leader of the United States of America.

Index

For main politician entries see contents page. References to politicians are given only where mentioned other than their main entry.

128